T0299236

Responsible Finance and Accounting

The UN Sustainable Development Goals, an increasing interest in Environmental, Social, and Governance factors, the climate crisis, stakeholder pressure, the lessons of corporate scandals, and the COVID-19 pandemic have triggered a massive change in how companies approach finance and accounting practices. From being a 'nice-to-have' to becoming a 'must-have', *Responsible Finance and Accounting* positions itself as a key pillar in tomorrow's better world for business, society, and planet.

In this book, leading researchers and practitioners in the field of corporate social responsibility, from the schools and corporate partners of the Council on Business & Society, give you key insights into green finance and social and environmental reporting, national, international, and corporate stakes in green taxonomy and carbon tax, and triple capital accounting. It also details how to model effective and low-cost social impact reporting, ethics in finance and accounting, and strategies for microfinance and finance-related social innovation. Each insight is accompanied by key takeaways, food for thought, and micro case study sections.

This accessible book will be a valuable resource for scholars, instructors, and upper-level students across finance and accounting as well as corporate social responsibility and business ethics. It will also serve as a guide for professionals aiming to deepen their understanding of new finance and accounting practice.

Adrián Zicari is Co-Head of the Accounting and Management Control Department at ESSEC Business School, Director of the Management and Society track, and Academic Director of the Council on Business & Society. He is also the Honorary representative for Buenos Aires in Paris. He holds a PhD in Management Administration from the Universidad Nacional de Rosario, an MBA (Universidad Adolfo Ibáñez), and a BSc in Accounting. Adrián's career has spanned the corporate sector as Financial Manager and Controller and his academic research has been widely published in leading journals, among others, *Journal of Business Ethics*, *Journal of Cleaner Production*, and *Social and Environmental Accountability Journal*.

Tom Gamble is Executive Director of the Council on Business & Society, running the operations, communications, and publications branches of the alliance. He holds an MA in Human Resource Management and Industrial Relations from Keele University as well as several coaching certifications. Tom's career has spanned teaching, lecturing, thought leadership, consulting, and instructional design, working with over 100 companies and educational institutions worldwide. He is a published author of fiction, non-fiction, and poetry.

Routledge CoBS Focus on Responsible Business
Series Editors: Tom Gamble and Adrián Zicari
The Council on Business and Society (CoBS)

This series is published in collaboration with the Council on Business & Society (CoBS).

Routledge CoBS Focus on Responsible Business provides international and multicultural perspectives on responsible leadership and business practices in line with the UN SDGs. Contributors from leading business schools on 4 continents offer local, cultural and global perspectives on the issues covered, drawing on high level research and transformed into engaging, and digestible content for students, academics and practitioners.

Topics include but are not limited to; responsible finance and accounting, CSR and governance, supply chain management, leadership, diversity and inclusion, performance and innovation, responsible management, and wellbeing at work.

Responsible Finance and Accounting
Performance and Profit for Better Business, Society and Planet
Edited by Adrián Zicari and Tom Gamble

Responsible Finance and Accounting

Performance and Profit for Better Business, Society and Planet

Edited by Adrián Zicari and Tom Gamble

With a Foreword by Professors Adrián Zicari and Annelise Vendramini Felsberg

LONDON AND NEW YORK

First published 2023
by Routledge
4 Park Square, Milton Park, Abingdon, Oxon OX14 4RN

and by Routledge
605 Third Avenue, New York, NY 10158

Routledge is an imprint of the Taylor & Francis Group, an informa business

British Library Cataloguing-in-Publication Data
A catalogue record for this book is available from the British Library

ISBN: 978-1-032-32918-5 (hbk)
ISBN: 978-1-032-32919-2 (pbk)
ISBN: 978-1-003-31733-3 (ebk)

DOI: 10.4324/9781003317333

Typeset in Times New Roman
by Apex CoVantage, LLC

For a wealthier, healthier, and greener world for all.

Contents

Contributors

In the order of appearance:

Prof. Annelise Vendramini Felsberg, FGV-EAESP GVces

Prof. Adrián Zicari, ESSEC Business School

Prof. Hugues Bouthinon-Dumas, ESSEC Business School

Prof. Qinqin Zheng, School of Management Fudan University

Prof. Aron Belinky, FGV-EAESP

Prof. Paulo D. Branco, FGV-EAESP

Prof. Savita Shankar, University of Pennsylvania

Ronald Rateiwa, Regional Economist for Southern Africa at IFC – International Finance Corporation

Prof. Meshach Aziakpono, Stellenbosch Business School

Prof. Charles H. Cho, Schulich School of Business, York University, Canada

Prof. Eduardo Henrique Diniz, FGV-EAESP

Prof. Antonio De Vito, IE Business School and Alma Mater University of Bologna

Prof. Charles H. Cho, Schulich School of Business, York University, Canada

Prof. Mark Christensen, ESSEC Business School Asia-Pacific

Prof. Sébastien Rocher, IAE Nancy School of Management

Raphaël Hara, Managing Director, Ksapa

Adrien Covo, ESG Analyst, Ksapa

Farid Baddache, CEO, Ksapa

Prof. Florence Cavélius, ESSEC Business School

Prof. Christoph Endenich, ESSEC Business School

Prof. Frederik Dahlmann, Warwick Business School

Prof. Anastasios Elemes, ESSEC Business School

Prof. Jeff Zeyun Chen, Neeley School of Business, Texas Christian University

Prof. Liliana Gelabert, IE Business School

Foreword

The book you are now beginning to read is the first one of a series of books, the *Routledge and CoBS Focus on Responsible Leadership*. As it happens with any first volume of a book series (or with the first number of a journal), the editors are full of hope. They have the legitimate hope of finding and nurturing an increasing readership for their nascent project. In the case of this book series, there are two additional reasons for hope. First, because this book series signals the consolidation and maturity of the Council on Business & Society (CoBS), a 10-year-old international alliance of business schools focused on corporate social responsibility (CSR), Sustainability, and the Common Good. Second, because the CoBS has an editorial style that combines practical insights, academic rigour, and a positive, constructive attitude to address the challenges of today. In short, hope is at the heart of its editorial line.

It is most appropriate that this book series begins with a book on Finance and Accounting. Not because we like these disciplines (disclaimer: one of us is a professor in Finance and the other in Accounting), but because both disciplines are indisputably at the core of the modern economic system. There is no way of addressing the multiple challenges of sustainability without the contribution of Finance and Accounting. Both are predominantly quantitative disciplines, with a reputation for being practical, close to reality, straightforward, and no-nonsense. If we want to bring about a substantive change to sustainability, these two disciplines are indispensable levers for such a change.

Finance is about the resources that are deployed in our economy. The essence of a financial analysis is the effort to understand and measure the consequences in the future of a decision made in the present, using forecasting and discount rates. In Finance, decisions cannot be detached from ethical considerations and thinking constantly about the future. As we well know, the choice of financing (i.e. providing material resources) to one project, to one activity instead of an alternative one, is not only a matter of calculations. Therefore, Finance as a discipline is well-equipped to discuss sustainability matters. And Accounting, as the universal language of business, matters as well. Measurement of corporate results, both financial and non-financial, is an unavoidable step for improving companies. If one cannot measure environmental and social impacts, the much-needed change in companies will not happen.

Consequently, this book provides a collection of insights with concrete, inspiring analyses. All of them are based on the latest academic research, both undertaken in the CoBS' member schools and in invited schools. These contributions, coming from five continents, represent different, complementary international perspectives.

In terms of content, the Finance chapter first explores why Finance plays a key role for the future of the planet. There are insights about green finance, the role of CSR in investment recommendations, and financial innovations in emerging markets, among other issues. The second part of the Finance chapter studies how Finance can change, and the impact of such a change on the financial profession, investors, and companies. Then, the Accounting chapter, in its first part, studies the role of the accounting profession in the ongoing transformation towards responsible and sustainable business models. There are insights about triple capital accounting, the green taxonomy, and green supply chain, among other issues. The second part of the Accounting chapter deals with ethics and sustainability leadership. For instance, there is an insight about how accounting firms influence their clients' moral conduct, and another on the results of greenwashing. As you may see, it is a wide, encompassing set of issues, bringing together some of the latest thought leadership in the field.

Welcome to our first book in the series. Hoping that you like it and that you accompany us in the coming volumes.

Dr. Annelise Vendramini, CFA, Professor at FGV, São Paulo
Dr. Adrián Zicari, Professor at ESSEC, Paris

1 Finance – a key role in the future of business, society, and the planet

A greener, responsible world of finance

Hugues Bouthinon-Dumas
ESSEC Business School

The times they are a changin'

We live in a world of constant change (from changing jobs, to laws affecting our driving habits, to new taxes, shifts in geopolitics, and the occurrence of natural disasters). Finance is central to these changes: it is both an industry affected by changes in the environment and itself a source of transformation in the world.

We might say that the wake-up call has been that of the climate crisis. Certainly, environmentalists, scientific experts, and even politicians advocated the need to address the damage done to nature long before 2018, but the role of Greta Thunberg, which at first sight may seem anecdotal, should not be underestimated. The young Swedish climate activist gained the world's attention by sitting outside the Swedish parliament and challenging the status quo to the extent that a massive shift in awareness and subsequent movement occurred throughout all walks of society – and of business too, including that of finance.

Leading figures such as Larry Fink, CEO of the influential investment management firm BlackRock, ex-Unilever CEO Paul Polman, and ex-Puma CEO Jochen Zeitz are heavyweight examples of business leaders too who have championed the cause of sustainability in their corporations and beyond. After all, players in the business and financial fields share the same planet as normal folks and do not forget that they have children too.

And early birds, ahead of their times, can also be counted such as Socially Responsible Investing – or SRI – funds, extra-financial rating agencies, or financial bodies seeking to win returns and at the same time do social or environmental good. In a French context, one such player is the AFD – the French Development Agency – a public institution that implements government policy in terms of fighting poverty and promoting sustainable development. However, such initiatives were few and with limited impact. What has triggered the shift towards green finance, in addition to acute awareness

DOI: 10.4324/9781003317333-2

of the urgency to tackle climate crisis, has been the astute use of both carrot and stick to get things moving faster. We see that the shift towards sustainability is also a question of solving coordination problems and therefore of adequate incentives.

Carrots and sticks

A carrot has come in the form of potential new investment opportunities and portfolios of financial products focusing on social and environmental stakes. A stick, perhaps more powerful in this instance, has come in the form of risk assessment.

Climate change with all the damage it causes and the social unrest that ensues have in large had a negative effect on financial institutions' assets. Take energy infrastructure that pollutes and contaminates the wider ecosystem of both the environment and businesses, or the recent examples of ski resorts which can no longer rely on regular or abundant snowfalls to attract their customers or investors.

In France too, the government has played an active – and major – role. In 2017, the Duty of Care law, or '*Loi sur le devoir de vigilance*' was adopted giving multinationals a legal obligation to identify and flag violation of human rights and the environment. Moreover, the law reaches out to firms' foreign subsidiaries and supply chains, thereby making it impossible for them to outsource social and environmental risks, or follow a business model that encourages unethical exploitation or harms the environment. For example, Rio Tinto's disputes with its shareholders and with Australian Aboriginal groups over the destruction of an Aboriginal sacred site show that large companies have little choice but to engage in a more virtuous and respectful corporate policy.

Sustainable finance – an elusive term

Sustainable, or Green, finance is a term that is wrought with ambiguity – mostly because the interests of players in the financial field for social and environmental matters vary greatly. However, what we can say is that sustainable finance has a concern for sustainable development and for long-term conciliation between economic, social, and environmental interests. It can be noted that the UN's use of the word sustainable with regard to a *sustainable company* moves away from a traditional separation of CSR and sustainable development within organisations to bring both the social and environmental dimensions under the one word – sustainability.

In a financial context, sustainable finance not only concerns products and initiatives relating to the energy transition or ecological efficiency but also encompasses topics such as social inequality, the digital divide, human rights and the fight against modern slavery, the protection and rights of minorities, gender equality, inclusivity, good governance, and the fight against corruption. In this light, rather than a fully fledged concept or set of practices, sustainable finance is more a trend that can be applied to various dimensions of 'sustainability' according to the context and interests of the financial player.

In some ways, sustainable finance could also be considered radical. A movement that aims to steer finance away from the short-term win to long-term development. And it is all-embracing, touching not only every segment in the finance field – banks, insurance companies, credit providers, pension and investment funds, private equity, and listed companies – but also the professions and fields that are satellite to it – such as regulators, auditors, rating agencies, and those in the legal profession.

Challenges and opportunities for the watchdogs

This shift towards green finance also impacts the legal practitioner and the regulator. Green bonds, for example, are essentially bonds, and green loans are primarily loans that have to be dealt with in the usual way. But the sustainable dimension added to these brings a whole new set of challenges and opportunities for the two professions.

Not least is how to qualify and check that a green bond is exactly that? And what sort of changes in contract does that engender? The rules of responsibility must also be defined to cater for the plethora of new financial products in the case of an issuer not keeping to his pledge to commit to environmentally friendly policy. Fiduciary obligation too has to be tackled, for contracts still seek maximum yield in the sole interest of their beneficiaries without taking into account the multiple dimensions of sustainability. Extra-financial reporting also has to come under the magnifying glass – for the information issuers included in their reports can be of varying degrees of relevance and interest. Here, some form of standardisation is called for and information presented in such a way as to make it clear and useful to all the stakeholders involved. And this leads to the question of compliance. What if a company breaches that compliance towards sustainable development? Can stakeholders and not only shareholders raise a red flag and file suit against the issuer?

Regulators too are faced with challenges. Traditionally, their remit consists in protecting savings and savers, keeping a watch over the markets and payments and ensuring the stability of the financial system to protect the economy. But regulators, as mentioned earlier, are humans and responsible citizens too – and have an interest in the issues and expectations of society as well as the role of government to provide impetus to sustainable development.

Recent years have seen much movement in the profession, with regulators launching partnerships both on a local and global level – the French AMF (French financial markets authority) joint initiative with the ACPR which deals with French prudential supervision, or the creation of the global NGFS (Network for Greening the Financial System) network.

Legal practitioners and regulators have a key role to provide the frameworks and vigilance for finance to walk the talk of sustainability, notably that of flagging and reacting to greenwashing and ensuring the integrity of markets against manipulations and insider operations. Together, with the financial professions, they form powerful leverage and a powerful dynamic for positive transition into a greener, more responsible finance.

Key takeaways

- Despite early initiatives such as SRI funds, sustainable finance has really only taken off in recent years following pressure from society (for example, Greta Thunberg) and business leaders (Larry Fink, Paul Polman, and Jochen Zeitz, among others).
- The dynamic has been caused by awareness of social and environmental issues and also by legislation that pushes firms to go sustainable, such as the French *Loi sur le devoir de vigilance* giving multinationals a legal obligation to identify and flag violation of human rights and the environment.
- Sustainable finance not only concerns products and initiatives relating to the energy transition but also encompasses topics such as social inequality, human rights, inclusivity, and good governance.
- Sustainable finance is a trend that can be applied to various dimensions of 'sustainability' according to the context and interests of the financial player.
- Sustainable finance aims to steer finance away from the short-term win to long-term development. It impacts every segment of the financial field and the professions that are satellite to it.
- Legal practitioners and regulators are seeing changes and opportunities in their professions. They have a key role in providing frameworks and vigilance in order to ensure that issuers walk the talk of sustainability.

Food for thought

- Should higher education institutions make 'sustainable finance' mandatory in the education they offer? If you are a full-time student or part-time executive participant, what aspects of this would you like to see in the curriculum?

- Think of the financial products you or your friends/family might have (e.g. insurance policies, stocks and shares, and savings accounts). On a scale of 1–5, to what extent do these cater to the social and environmental transition? Among those that clearly claim to be 'sustainable', how much trust do you place in them to walk the talk? Why? Why not?
- According to you, what should come first to make sustainable finance work? A change in people's values and behaviour or a change in law and regulations to change the sector?
- To what extent will finance always be concerned with profit first? Is it naïve to think otherwise?

Related work: *The Sustainable Finance and Law Conference, La Sorbonne, October 22, 2019, ESSEC Business School within the framework of the RTDBF (Réseau transnational de droit bancaire et financier/ Transnational Network on Banking and Financial Law).*

With heart and head

How to bring them together for sustainable investment decisions

Qinqin Zheng
School of Management Fudan University

Imagine a fund manager, employed by a pension fund, an insurance company. Imagine too, any investor willing to place some of her own savings. Both belong to an increasing number of 'conscious investors' – aware of the impact that business has on society and the planet. And with a goal to ensure that their money is invested in companies that are sound in terms of their ethical, social, and environmental footprint. Their challenge is knowing where to best invest.

On the other side of the coin is the company seeking investors. Their aim is to ensure positive corporate financial performance. Their challenge is knowing how to attract investors.

Is there a link between the two challenges? And if so, what brings them together?

Nothing is simple

Although past research has found that there is indeed a link between how a company walks the talk of corporate social performance (CSP) and positive corporate financial performance (CFP), there is still a lasting – and controversial – debate as to the degree of influence the former has on the latter.

Indeed, one of the complexities is that of CSP itself. What is it? How is it measured? And how do potential investors know how and where to identify if a company does good? Or, moreover, if that company is simply greenwashing through a cool and energetic green marketing strategy?

The answer partly lies in ratings carried out by professionals such as Thomson Reuters and KLD. But the information can be voluminous, detailed, and too complicated for generalists to quickly grasp. And too multidimensional to offer a clear yes or no investment scenario. Going back to the insurance firm wishing to invest, you might think that it would be able to see through the mist. But they too have their challenges, research pointing to one of the largest of them being a simple lack of time and resources.

DOI: 10.4324/9781003317333-3

And it gets more complicated

Another dimension that adds to the challenge is that of shareholder versus stakeholder theory. Back in 1970, the economist Milton Friedman published an essay in which he stated that the social responsibility of a business is to increase profit and reward its core investors – its shareholders – with returns on their investment in the company. This thinking still presides today and there are many examples of companies that aim for maximum profit and returns in order to handsomely reward their investors. The problem is that in doing so, some of these companies might overlook the impact their profit-at-all-cost approach has on people and the planet.

In 1984, Prof. Ed Freeman countered shareholder theory with stakeholder theory, contending that business also had an additional, ethical responsibility of taking into account its links and relationships with customers, employees, suppliers, investors, and communities impacted by the company's activities. In recent years, many have claimed that the environment also constitutes a further – important – 'stakeholder'. Freeman argues that the primary goal of a business is to create value for all its stakeholders, not just its shareholders.

The media coverage of financial scandals, breaches of conduct, poor working conditions of outsourced production and supply chain resources in developing countries, and pollution levels has meant that potential shareholders increasingly see corporate social performance as important. Not only does a good and clean record do good for the various stakeholders in a company's ecosystem, it also attracts investors and adds additional value to stocks and shares and thus returns.

But here too, it is difficult for potential investors to pinpoint who or what belongs to a company's ecosystem of stakeholders and what effect the company's business activities have on them.

An unsuspecting hero

Behold the unsuspecting heroes – the stock and security analysts. Their jobs contain a lot of research on financial and extra-financial data, analysis of this, and ultimately advice and recommendations for investment decisions. They are also certified experts who are skilled at rooting out private information and, as such, are in a good position to assess the value of a firm in terms of corporate social performance.

The security analyst plays a mediatory role between the firm and investors, acting much like an information bridge. To check this, research carried out has analysed information revealed in surveys of 388 fund managers carried out by Deloitte, CSR Europe, and Euronext in the early

2000s – those responsible for investing decisions – and security analysts. The insights gleaned were that a high proportion of analysts are aware of CSR-related information and consider it important. The results also highlighted the tendency of analysts to integrate corporate social performance information in their reports to provide potential investors with buy or sell recommendations.

Indeed, 79% of fund managers and analysts in the survey indicated that the social responsibility dimension has a long-term positive impact on a company's value, with 51% of fund managers and 37% of financial analysts granting a stock price premium to firms showing good practice in corporate social responsibility.

Investors too are increasingly reported to be citing CSR-related issues when discussing with financial institutions for advice on where to put their money – with particular interest in poor working conditions, corruption, human rights violations, and environmental destruction.

Analysts lean on tools and databases to help them. For the former dimensions, one source is RepRisk, while RobecoSAM caters for sustainability or impact investing. Further insights can be obtained from searching a firm's ISO accreditation. ISO-14001 and OHSAS-18001 are particularly relevant as they reward exceptionally high standards in occupational health and safety management.

Analysts are also a thorough brand of professional, with a tendency to include in their reports factors such as product impact on the environment, its quality, employee relations, governance, corporate outreach, and impact on communities as well as keeping an eye out for a company's use of green tech or new and eco-friendly practices, be it wastewater processing or solar panels for reusable energy.

Survey interviews highlighted the fact that even if analysts know that a firm's stock is undervalued, they refrain from recommending a buy if the firm is likely to receive a negative CSR assessment.

Of heart and head

All in all, findings point to analysts holding a pivotal role as intermediaries, and the most apt at clearing the mist in understanding the volume and complexity of information involved when assessing the CSP of a firm. To a great extent, they also serve as providers of win–win recommendations to investors – ensuring logical investment with profitable returns, while checking that the investment is made in a socially and environmentally responsible company. In short, bringing shareholder and stakeholder theory together. And, why not, offering a decision that can be made by both head and heart at once.

Key takeaways

- Research has shown that there is a link between a company's corporate social performance (CSP) and corporate financial performance (CFP).
- CSR performance is increasingly important for all investors, not only socially responsible ones.
- There is an increasing number of 'conscious investors' who want to ensure that their money is invested in companies that are sound in terms of their ethical, social, and environmental footprint.
- The challenge for generalist investors is that information on CSP is complex to decipher in order to make investment decisions.
- The complexity is deepened with the advent of stakeholder theory – where the primary goal of a business is to create value for all its stakeholders – as opposed to shareholder theory.
- Research points to the solution lying in the role of the security analyst (sometimes called stock or financial analyst), specialised in research and skilled at accessing private information to make recommendations to potential investors.
- In-depth exploration of financial analysts' work shows that the CSR dimension is an important factor in their recommendations.
- As such, financial analysts hold a pivotal role as intermediaries and 'bridges' between CSR performance and corporate value.

Food for thought

- To what extent do you personally think corporate social performance is an important factor for investors? Should investors focus purely on return on investment?
- How does your own organisation fare in terms of CSR initiatives and policy? How do they add value – if any – to your organisation?
- To what extent do you think that companies who do not show a good record in CSR and environmental impact should be penalised on the stock exchange? How?

Related research: *Corporate Social Performance, Analyst Stock Recommendations, and Firm Future Returns. Strategic Management Journal, Strat. Mgmt. J., 36: 123–136 (2015). DOI: 10.1002/smj*

CSR and sustainability indexes

A virtuous circle

Adrián Zicari
ESSEC Business School

Awareness of the urgent need to address both social and environmental issues has led to a surge of interest in SRI – or socially responsible investing. Also known as ethical or green investing, SRI presents a win–win for the potential investor. As with traditional investing, it aims to gain a financial return for the investor, while also ensuring that the investor's money is spent on firms seeking to demonstrate a commitment to improving their positive impact on business operations – including working conditions, society, and planet.

This is all very well, and admirably so, but the challenge remains for the investor to know exactly what the firm's record is in terms of responsible business practices in order to make a decision to invest. It is here that the sustainability index – with stocks quoted in terms of ESG (environmental, social, and governance) criteria – becomes relevant.

Developed in the north, innovated in the south

Although widely espoused today, sustainability isn't something new and neither are sustainability indexes. Spurred by the UN Global Impact of 1999, they began to feature in industrialised and developed countries shortly after – the US Dow Jones Sustainability Index of 1999 and the UK FTSEGood index of 2001 are shining examples that are often quoted when criticising developing and emerging economies where such indexes are lacking.

But this moral stance on the part of developed countries may not be entirely justified. First and foremost because such indexes indeed appeared in the US and UK at a mature stage in their markets, and secondly because developing markets are indeed trying to make good by developing their own. There is, however, a difference – emerging markets tending to tailor their indexes to local contexts and conditions, while at the same time addressing the comparatively low liquidity of their markets and lowering

DOI: 10.4324/9781003317333-4

the cost for the investor in terms of obtaining correct and affirmed information required for their investment decisions. A leader in this field is Latin America, and more specifically Brazil, Chile, Mexico, and Argentina.

A model of difference

The way sustainability indexes have developed in these countries differs from those of richer economies. They also provide an approach that is a useful benchmark for other emerging countries in the region or elsewhere such as Africa or parts of Asia. Indeed, the surge in interest of such indexes in developing economies is remarkable – and a sure sign that interest in responsible business is not only limited to the wealthier economies of this world. Moreover, the situation in Latin America contrasts notably with those of developed markets where SRI has become a relatively common investment practice. In 2020, for example, a third of the value invested in professionally managed assets in the US was due to sustainability investment strategy (US SIF, 2020).

A major difference in the context of Latin America is that their stock markets are less liquid and tend to be concentrated in a few companies. Another difference with developed markets is that environmental, social, and governance-related (ESG) data can be scarce and not systematically collected. As such, the cost of obtaining ESG data can become prohibitive for aspiring investors in socially responsible firms in the region.

Consequently, many stock exchanges in Latin America have created their own sustainability indexes, with the objective of gaining a critical mass of SRI investors. Brazil, Mexico, Chile, and Argentina have shown creativity and Latin flair by detouring this costly option – creating indexes via their local stock markets and distributing ESG data at no cost for the investor to use.

Brazil

Brazil is of particular interest and in the vanguard of socially responsible investing – not only locally, but internationally. As long ago as 2005, the São Paulo stock exchange created the ISE (now called ISE B3) corporate sustainability index, effectively the fourth such index in the world and the second to have been created in an emerging market.

Its operating mechanism merits a detour, as well as its impact. ESG data is collected on a voluntary basis, corresponding to a gamut of criteria: general, product nature, corporate governance, economic and finance, environmental, social, and climate change. Before a firm is allowed to enter the index, it must meet two prerequisites – that of having a good score in the seven criteria stated earlier and that of having a minimum level of liquidity.

In terms of results, the Brazilian ISE B3 does not offer starkly different returns than those of a traditional portfolio. However, it can be argued that SRI investors still prefer to place their money in companies with better ESG performance. Nonetheless, the ISE B3 index can claim to have a direct impact and influence on corporate practice, attracting firms aiming to build their reputations through their presence on the index, thus making their good practice visible, gleaning knowledge and influence.

Mexico and Chile

After an initial experience in 2011, the Mexican stock exchange launched a new sustainability index in 2020, together with Standard & Poor's. The S&P/BMV Total Mexico ESG Index now includes 29 companies. Again launched by its national stock exchange, the sustainability index for the Chilean market was jointly launched with the S&P Dow Jones and known under the name of the Dow Jones Sustainability Index Chile (DJSI Chile). Something that sets both experiences apart is the partnership with an international firm.

Argentina

The Argentinean stock exchange launched its sustainability index in 2019, with the support of the IDB (Inter-American Development Bank). It is a different methodology that takes into consideration not only ESG (Environmental, Social, and Governance) elements but also the contribution of the company to the development of the region. With this methodology, the Buenos Aires Stock Exchange presents a list of chosen companies. For instance, there were 15 firms for the 2020 version of this index. The index is rebalanced every year.

Decision time

For investors, the most important information in order to make their investment decision is not how the index is composed, but the methodology for assessing ESG performance. For instance, a 'best-in-class' approach may meet with resistance from some investors. Controversial businesses such as oil may still be listed on the indexes. And as only the top firms are selected, many firms with healthy responsible business reputations are prone to lose out and remain hidden from the screen.

As such, sustainability indexes cannot perfectly replace ESG rating agencies. Moreover, both serve varying purposes – the indexes are used as references and benchmarks for SRI portfolios, while rating agencies assess the ESG performance of specific firms. That being said, the information present in the Latin American Sustainability Indexes still provides a good deal of assistance to SRI investors to make their decisions – responsibly.

Key takeaways

- SRI (socially responsible investing) aims to gain a financial return for the investor, while also ensuring that the investor's money is spent on firms seeking to demonstrate a commitment to improving their positive impact on business operations, society, and planet.
- Sustainability indexes, with stocks quoted in terms of ESG (environmental, social, and governance) criteria help potential investors in their investment decisions.
- Spurred by the UN Global Impact of 1999, sustainability indexes were created in developed countries, for example, the US Dow Jones Sustainability Index of 1999 and the UK FTSEGood index of 2001.
- Some Latin American countries, such as Brazil, Mexico, Chile, and Argentina, have created indexes, though they function differently.
- A major difference with developed markets is that Latin American stock exchanges participate directly with the objective of gaining a critical mass of respected and reputable stakeholders, through combining the limited nature of stock exchanges on the continent and the high cost of obtaining ESG data.
- In Brazil, the São Paulo stock exchange created the ISE (now ISE B3) sustainability index in 2005. ESG data is collected on a voluntary basis, with seven assessment criteria: general, product nature, corporate governance, economic and finance, environmental, social, and climate change. A firm must obtain a good score in the seven criteria and have a minimum level of liquidity.
- The ISE index has a direct impact and influence on corporate practice: reputation, visibility for good practice, and influence among competitors and suppliers.
- Both the Mexican and the Chilean stock exchanges have sustainability indexes, in both cases in partnership with S&P Dow Jones. The Argentinean stock exchange has also launched its sustainability index, with the support of the IDB.

Food for thought

- What are your views on the Latin American models of sustainability indexes? To what extent are they a viable alternative to paying for data from rating agencies?
- Should such an initiative be widened to include SMEs? Why and how?
- Why would you personally put money – or not – in socially responsible investments?

References

Related Research: *Sustainability Indices in Latin America: Can Financial Markets Push for CSR? Concepts, Perspectives and Emerging Trends in Ibero-America*, https://doi.org/10.1108/S2043-052320170000011001

US SIF (2020) *Sustainable and Impact Investing – Overview*, accessed from www. ussif.org, March 2022

Zicari (2020) *L'ISR en Amérique Latine: un développement via les indices?* In *ISR & Finance Responsable*, N. Mottis (Ed.). Chapter 9, Ellipses, Paris

Micro case study 1: Finance

It is Tuesday afternoon. Tea time. But today you do not have time for tea. Indeed, you do not know whether it is sunny or not outside, as you've been in the office all day working hard. Your employer is a traditional, very respected private bank where you are a financial advisor. You advise the bank's clients on their long-term investments. You have a reputation for being a reliable, knowledgeable professional, always attentive to your clients' expectations.

Today you have a meeting with a new client, Mr. Dupont-Dupont. He is a retired member of the diplomatic service and has been ambassador to several countries. While not rich, he has some savings that he wants to invest wisely. As you always do, you begin to collect information about your new client's expectations and needs. This information is indispensable for preparing an investment policy tailored to your new client's needs. At some point in the conversation, while you enumerate some alternatives for investment, Mr. Dupont-Dupont looks into your eye and tells you: 'Of course, do not even think of green investments, social responsibility or the like. Everybody knows that all that stuff is pure marketing'.

Maybe yes, maybe not, you think to yourself. Indeed, you have been learning about green investments. Indeed, you're now reading a very nice book, *Responsible Finance and Accounting*. It is a fairly new, but growing tendency that is becoming mainstream. You feel that there are some arguments that your client should be aware of, despite his reluctance to green finance.

What can you tell your client about green investments? Do they make sense for an individual investor to keep an eye on them? Are they promising? More or less interesting than conventional investments? More or less risky? Is it a path worth exploring?

Brazil and the ISE B3 index
A focus on sustainability pioneering, its creation, and challenges

Aron Belinky and Paulo D. Branco
FGV-EAESP

Launched in 2005, the fourth in the world and the second in an emerging economy, the ISE B3 index confirmed Brazil's position as a pioneer in corporate sustainability. Now in its seventeenth consecutive portfolio, its roots go back to 2003 when the Bovespa, the São Paulo stock exchange as it was named at that time – now B3 – began initial discussions with ABN Amro bank, itself is known as a pioneer in the creation of ethical funds in Brazil. ABN Amro was then exploring the idea of a CSR-related fund to benchmark its performance.

The pioneering role of the ISE B3 was also part of a deeper surge in interest for sustainability in the early 2000s, when a new generation of Brazilian business leaders began championing a number of social-environmental initiatives. These were concentrated for the most part in organisations such as Instituto Ethos, helping businesses to manage their operations in a socially responsible manner; the Fundação Abrinq, an NGO working in the fields of children's rights and inclusive education; and the IBGC – the Brazilian Institute for Corporate Governance – among others.

Every seed needs fertile ground, that of the ISE B3 being the re-democratisation of Brazil in the mid-1980s after more than two decades of military regime, the Rio Conference of 1992, the World Bank's social and environmental Millennium Development Goals in Y2K, and the third UN Conference on Sustainable Development – Rio+20 – held in Brazil in 2012. Added to this was the key role played by the modernisation of the country's capital market and banking system.

In this light, the ISE B3 index is deep-rooted in participative, democratic, and sustainability values which still now, nearly 20 years on and despite a general rise in populist and counter-values in recent years, underlies the unique approach of the index and which sets it apart from others around the globe. Despite the social-environmental regressive agenda pushed by the Brazilian federal government since 2019, the commitment of leading

DOI: 10.4324/9781003317333-5

business and financial system actors improved the capital market. Betterments came, for instance, from the country's regulatory agency (CVM) and the Brazilian Central Bank (BACEN), which updated and enhanced several policies and instruments favourable to more sustainable investment and better market information. Indeed, the country still retains a sizeable body of business-sector players working hand-in-hand with civil society, educational institutes, and governmental sectors striving to keep to the sustainability agenda and move things forward. It is likely too that the ISE B3 will remain a pioneer, innovator, and flagbearer of sustainability in the private sector in the future.

An index – with a difference

In line with what has been agreed under Agenda 2030 and its SDGs – as well as older frameworks such as ISO26000, the Paris Agreement, and the Global Reporting Initiative – most global stock exchanges focus essentially on the same aspects. More recently, the hype involving the ESG agenda (acronym for Environmental, Social, and Governance) has increased the demand for standardisation on corporate sustainability information. This accelerated dialogue and the building of common ground between key actors, such as GRI (the Global Reporting Initiative) and SASB (the Sustainability Accounting Standards Board), among many others. Nevertheless, the approaches regarding business's relation with sustainability are still very diverse. In such a context, the ISE B3 sets itself apart in terms of methodology and working approach. First, it is important to highlight that the ISE B3 is not just a rating agency measuring individual companies' sustainability performance. Although companies are rated as part of the selection process, the index itself is the indicator of the change in value of a portfolio composed of company shares selected and based on how well they incorporate sustainability in their strategies, policies, and practices.

This selection is based on the combination of a broad, voluntary questionnaire submitted to companies, which they fill out themselves, with information provided by independent sources. The information gleaned is analysed in both absolute and relative terms. The way the questionnaire itself is developed is also highly original, going through a process of continuous improvement and update through public debate and bringing together the participation of companies and their ecosystem of stakeholders. As such, this guarantees that the agenda remains well-founded as well as incorporating expectations as to what the business world must do to achieve social and environmental good.

In addition to the questionnaire, ISE B3's selection process features a qualitative documental check on a random sample of each company's answers.

This provides an idea of the likely credibility of their general answers to the questionnaire. The quality of such evidence impacts the company's overall score, and those with bad performance in this checking phase are less likely to be selected for the portfolio. In addition, a company's answers are published, thereby allowing for public scrutiny of its statements. Stakeholders may indeed question the validity of a company's answers, which can result in the company being required to leave the ISE B3's portfolio if misalignment occurs. It is this – the transparency of the ISE B3 – that is also a key factor shaping its success and uniqueness.

Finally, it is important to point out that ISE B3's method of selection is not simply a mathematical algorithm. Indeed, the entire process keeps track of each company's performance in six different sustainability dimensions: human capital, corporate governance and high management, business model and innovation, social capital, environment, and climate change. The company cannot balance out a poor score in one dimension with positive scores in others. This multidimensional perspective has been adopted by ISE B3 since its beginning and has been adapted over the years. The current division, adopted in 2021, is aligned to the SASB's framework, reflecting the movement towards a more even terminology and approach in the field. Nevertheless, ISE B3 still preserve its uniqueness and compatibility with the Brazilian context, captured in the more granular level of its questionnaire.

Another important change happened in ISE B3's methodology reform implemented in 2021. Until then, the selection process culminated in an in-depth debate at the level of ISE B3's Deliberative Board composed of representatives of 11 institutions or organisations firmly anchored in various sectors relating to ISE's agenda. While stakeholders still have an important role in annual review of the questionnaire, the final decision-making process became more transparent and objective. Harnessing on the advent of Big Data, the final check by the board of experts has been replaced by a combination of criteria, including external and independent assessment on certain aspects. A reputational perspective is provided by RepRisk, a global ESG risks information provider, and the climate change dimension assessment comes straight from CDP, who partnered with B3 to improve the selection process, streamline assessment criteria, and reduce companies reporting burden.

Challenges and lessons

Setting up ISE B3 and managing to keep it running for almost 18 consecutive years has in many ways been a challenge. On a technical side, various obstacles have had to be overcome regarding the scoring methodology, developing the selection process algorithm, and the IT system to support it all.

However, perhaps the most challenging aspect has been the series of discussions – indeed negotiations – on the structure and content of the questionnaire handed to companies, as well as obtaining the commitment of companies and other stakeholders. In the early days, scepticism was one major issue to solve. On another dimension, NGOs and unions were especially wary of the risk of greenwashing. On the other hand, less engaged or excessively pragmatic corporate players saw the whole thing as a time-consuming and attention-dispersing adventure that carried with it the risk of creating conflict with traditionally prudent stakeholders. The proliferation of ESG instruments and poorly-based claims of sustainable performance added an extra layer to such debate.

The credibility of FGV, Brazil's premier academic institution involved with developing the index, was an important factor in swinging opinion, as was the even more crucial transparency and adherence to a clear, open, and well-intentioned process. As such, it was the essential ingredients of trust and dialogue which enabled various stakeholders to co-construct a common agenda and process to firmly support the ISE B3. The same attitude was kept during ISE B3's 2020 reform, conducted directly by B3 and its current technical partner (ABC Associados, a consultancy firm by former FGV researchers).

One downside of ISE B3 is that there is no formal evaluation of its impact, although clear evidence exists of its relevance to companies, wider society, and the market. Such evidence includes the fluctuations in a company's share value depending on whether or not it features in the ISE B3 portfolio, the actions and narrative of business leaders and their staff in terms of responsible business practice, as well as certain aspects of corporate performance. Moreover, endorsement of the ISE B3 index has come in the form of frequent citation by the business world, professionals, academia, the media, and government bodies as a reference for corporate sustainability.

For companies participating in the ISE B3 index, the selection process is in itself an opportunity for them to carry out self-assessment, diagnosis, and planning in sustainability-related matters.

Proper naming

The terminology around sustainability is rife. The phrase 'ethical investment' – predominant two decades ago when the ISE B3 was created and still used by many – is perhaps not the most relevant term to describe what ISE B3 and other similar indexes are all about. 'Ethical' might carry the notion of moral judgement on certain types of sector and business. While this could be the case of pension funds managed by religious institutions, it cannot be applied to many others and certainly leads to lower potential for mainstreaming and scaling up. On the other hand, the current buzzword – ESG – is being used as 'fit-for-all' phrase, but with no actual meaning. Adding 'ESG' to qualify a company, investment or methodology tells us nothing except that it is touching environmental, social, or governance aspects in its actions or decisions. By itself, it has no actual value or implications for sustainability or competitiveness.

'Sustainable investment', 'responsible', 'green', or even 'social investment' might be more relevant alternatives, the overarching argument being that the world is moving towards a more or less rapid transition to an entirely different business environment set off by a combination of technological, environmental, cultural, and demographic transformations. 'Impact investing', another trending phrase related to similar issues, brings a different perspective, basically the intentionality of combining positive externalities with value creation for the firm. It's not yet the case of stock exchange indexes such as ISE B3, which deals with mainstream firms.

The emerging profile of sustainable investment means not simply looking at companies that do good but trying to sort out those who are catching up with the transition – and, as such, contributing to a fairer and more sustainable world. And secondly, looking at those who procrastinate – companies unable or unwilling to revamp their businesses – or are too anchored in their past or current comfort, despite their incompatibility with the new and sustainable context in which they find themselves. There is clear evidence of how responsible investors react to such cases – removing their investment in carbon-intensive portfolios, dumping stranded assets, and searching for innovative new businesses with a sustainable impact. Far from a passing trend, sustainability investment is here to stay – for a faster, cleaner, and brighter future.

Key takeaways

* The ISE B3 sustainability index was created in a context of a new generation of business leaders championing a number of social-environmental initiatives; the re-democratisation of Brazil in the mid-1980s; landmark international conferences on sustainability held in Brazil; and the modernisation of the country's capital market and banking system.
* The ISE B3 is different from other indexes in terms of methodology and working approach. It is an indicator of the change in value of a portfolio composed of company shares selected and based on how well they incorporate sustainability in their strategies, policies, and practices.

- Each company's performance is gauged on six different sustainability dimensions, recently aligned to the SASB's framework: human capital, corporate governance and high management, business model and innovation, social capital, environment, and climate change. As such, this allows for a multiperspective view of the firm.
- Transparency is a key factor to ISE B3's success and uniqueness. Companies reply to a questionnaire on a voluntary basis, which goes through a process of continuous improvement and update through public and stakeholder scrutiny and debate.
- Companies are then asked to supplement an initial assessment to obtain a final score. On top of the above-threshold scoring – both overall and on every applicable issue – other requirements must be fulfilled regarding the company's reputation and the quality of the evidence provided to back its answers to the questionnaire.
- The emerging profile of sustainable investment means not simply looking at companies that do good but trying to sort out those who are catching up with the transition and those who lag in their efforts to become responsible.

Food for thought

- Should every company in a country's economy be subject to sustainability assessment? Why? Why not?
- In what ways can governments or industry associations reward companies that demonstrate a dynamic sustainability policy?
- How would your own company, organisation, or institution rate on a similar sustainability index? What would you improve?

Can non-banking financial institutions help Africa reach the SDGs?

Ronald Rateiwa and Meshach Aziakpono
Stellenbosch Business School

The 2030 agenda for sustainable development that gave birth to the 17 UN SDGs (sustainable development goals) adopted in 2015 has provided the world with a framework and target to make business, society, and planet cleaner and fairer, more inclusive, and greener. These are ambitions that are noble in nature and urgent to address. However, there is a hitch. Quite apart from awareness, a change in attitude, behaviour, and commitment on a global scale, there is also the question of the financial resources and infrastructure needed to achieve the aspirations encapsulated in the SGDs.

Some countries – the developed economies – seem to have a head start. Others – emerging economies or developing countries – would seem to have a harder challenge ahead of them to fulfil the SDG goals. Added to that, both in more affluent and less wealthy countries, the shadow of the global financial crisis of 2007–2009 still lingers. The shock waves may have abated, but the ripples still remain, and were exacerbated by the COVID-19 pandemic which disrupted financial flows and supply value chains. Wary of the risks of fragile financial markets, bank lending has largely slowed. This is not good news, as long-term financing is required to support development and solutions to reach the SDGs, at a time when government fiscal capacity has remained constrained.

As such, the emerging economies have to seek resources elsewhere. And this is where the non-banking financial institutions – or NBFIs – come in as an alternative. Or maybe even as a saviour.

NBFIs and Africa

NBFIs are financial institutions without a full banking licence and therefore cannot take deposits. However, they can provide other financial services such as savings in the form of insurance policies, pension, and mutual

DOI: 10.4324/9781003317333-6

funds, or microloans and investment possibilities such as venture capital for budding start-ups.

Can the development of such institutions help Africa? In order to answer the question, it is necessary to look into whether or how they have influenced economic growth on the continent and what could be done to improve their respective financial systems to give them a boost.

Significant leaders in Africa's collective economy and financial system are Egypt, South Africa, and Nigeria – whose NBFIs mainly operate in insurance, pension funds, and investment firms. They provide an interesting basis for investigation for a number of reasons. Not only do the three countries have the oldest capital markets on the continent – making it practical to study data over time – the trio also accounts for 60% of all infrastructure investments in Africa, in large part funded by NBFIs. As leaders, they can provide insight and examples on how best to tweak policy in other African countries.

The challenge

However, not everyone views NBFIs with rose-tinted glasses. The financial crisis of 2007–2008 saw the headlines featuring various financial institutions as the cause of the collapse, the most famous perhaps being the investment bank Lehman Brothers, its 25,000 employees worldwide seeing their jobs go up in smoke in a matter of a day. The lesson learnt was that if the development of non-financial banking institutions is too fast, and incorrectly regulated and monitored, they can create the conditions for a financial crisis to take place.

Indeed, studies and reports have since brought attention to two major factors that countries would be wise to consider when contemplating measures to boost the presence of NBFIs in their markets. The first is linked to loose regulations that may fail to harness excessive NBFI appetite for risk, which imperils the financial sector and the real economy. And secondly, although NBFIs do contribute to the real economy, they can become a source of risk if they both perform functions traditionally carried out by banks, and their ways of operating are too interconnected to them.

A further issue is that the assumption that financial development is directly linked to economic growth is being challenged. Here too, studies have shown that the relationship between the two is weakening both in developed and developing countries – suggesting that long-term economic growth is not as influenced by finance as it once was.

This all calls into question the role and impact of NBFIs in helping Africa to meet the UN SDGs. Does the development of these NBFIs follow demand – that is, does economic growth lead to financial development? Or do they supply-lead, acting as a locomotive that pulls growth forward and precedes the real economy?

At first glance, the latter seems the most logical – financial development easing the savings and efficient allocation of capital, which in turn generates economic growth. A counterargument, however, is that financial development decreases or does away with the limits set on the amount of money that can be borrowed – thereby reducing the incentive to save and thus, in this case, restricting economic growth.

A third avenue to explore is that NBFIs follow both demand and lead supply simultaneously – a two-way scenario that takes place in either a vicious or virtuous cycle. In the first case, economic growth is so low that it prevents growth in the financial sector, which in turn prevents economic growth. Therefore, the effect of development on the number and impact of NBFIs would be negative. On the other hand, a virtuous cycle in which a high level of economic growth encourages the development of the financial sector, in turn, stimulating even more growth in the economy, would see a positive impact for NBFIs in the long term.

The results

In-depth research on the financial development, growth in NBFIs, and economic performance of Egypt, Nigeria, and South Africa have yielded a number of interesting and useful findings.

In Egypt, the evidence gleaned from data between 1980 and 2017 shows that the effect of NBFIs on economic growth in the country is both positive and significant. On a demand side, growing the economy has generated far more development in the financial sector, which generates even more economic growth. This means that a virtuous cycle exists, NBFIs and economic growth mutually strengthening each other.

In Nigeria, the picture is more mixed. Although research results point to a weak relationship between NBFI development and economic growth, there is a sufficient glimmer of light to suggest that NBFIs can have a say in pushing the economy forward.

And in South Africa, findings show that the development of NBFIs stimulates economic growth, suggesting that the link between the two is essentially supply-leading – NBFIs create financial products in advance that are required by the economy and thereby facilitating economic development. The relationship is positive and long term.

In a nutshell, Egypt and South Africa come up with stronger results and arguments for the place and role NBFIs have to play. This might not come as a surprise, both countries taking the claim of possessing the most developed financial systems on the continent where the impact of NBFIs is more salient. Put another way, this means that countries would do well to develop policies aimed at boosting the development of NBFIs given their potential to help the economy grow.

But the results also show lacunas in the three countries' financial systems, as well as rigidity in their economies. However, where there are weaknesses, there are also opportunities to improve and grow stronger.

Improving the efficiency of the financial system in Egypt is first on the menu, and here policies can be developed and implemented to enable the system to better carry out its role of aligning savings holders with borrowers through banks and other third parties. This improved intermediation will undoubtedly boost economic growth given the strong, positive impact of NBFI development on the country's economy.

For Nigeria, it may be a different picture. With a weak, long-term influence of NBFIs on Nigeria's economy, external factors seem to influence the finance–growth relationship more than anything else. There is a need for policies that create an enabling environment for growth. Once up and running, and the economy reaching a certain level of performance, they will create a virtuous growth cycle. The legal system especially needs bolstering and strengthening, guaranteeing property rights and helping to ensure the proper improvement of roads and electricity supply. Nigeria is also over-reliant on its oil and gas industry which in 2019 was calculated to bring in 65% of the country's revenues. The government has made an effort to diversify the economy with mining and agriculture, and this must continue in future years.

Finally, South Africa. Here, faced with a general drop in bank lending, the rise of the NBFI has emerged as an alternative source of long-term capital and research results point to the need to encourage the development of these institutions further. However, in parallel, regulatory frameworks have to be tightened to avoid drift and excessive risk – thereby avoiding financial crises in the country and beyond. 2030 is fast approaching. And while NBFIs might not amount to almighty saviours, they at least might create a few minor miracles.

Key takeaways

- The 2030 agenda for sustainable development pushes countries to reach the objectives set by the UN SDGs.
- Countries require capital to finance initiatives and developments for this. But the world financial crisis has meant a decline in banks' lending money.
- As such, emerging economies must turn to alternative means to raise resources. NBFIs may be the solution.

- Lessons from the financial crisis show that if the development of NBFIs is too fast, and incorrectly regulated and monitored, they can create the conditions for a financial crisis to occur.
- The link between NBFIs and economic growth is not systematically established. The development of NBFIs can follow demand – economic growth leading to financial development; or supply-lead, acting as a locomotive for economic growth; or follow demand and lead supply simultaneously, creating virtuous or vicious cycles.
- In Egypt, the effect of NBFIs on economic growth in the country is both positive and significant.
- In Nigeria, there is a weak relationship between NBFI development and economic growth, due to external factors influencing the system, loose regulation, and legal frameworks.
- In South Africa, NBFIs stimulate economic growth, and their development is essentially supply-leading. The relationship is positive and long term.

Food for thought

- How do you see the economic development of Africa? To what extent is it a continent to be reckoned with in the next 50 to 100 years?
- If you were leading a government in an African country, what four major policies would you implement to stimulate i) growth in start-ups, ii) growth in innovation, iii) the development of NBFIs to serve them, and iv) more involvement of NBFIs in infrastructure development?
- Which SDGs do you think Africa could reach more easily by 2030? Which represent major challenges? What can be done to overcome these challenges?

Related research: Non-bank Financial Institutions and Economic Growth: Evidence From Africa's Three Largest Economies, May 2017, South African Journal of Economic and Management Sciences (SAJEMS) 20(1), DOI: 10.4102/sajems.v20i1.1545

Micro case study 2: Finance

Monday morning in Puerto Madero, at the heart of the business district in Buenos Aires. You are in a large room, with a magnificent view of the River Plate. Today, it is your first day as a member of the investment committee of the NAIRDA Bank, a large, prestigious (and indeed fictitious) bank in Argentina. The investment committee is at the core of the bank's strategy. Its role is to define the long-term investment policy for the bank. Mrs. López Guerrero, the committee president, starts the discussion: 'Ladies and gentlemen, we need to revise our investment policy. Inflation is increasing and many of our investments are not as profitable as we expected. And then we have a group of shareholders asking us to include ESG considerations in our portfolio. For instance, some of them are worried about our investments in oil and tobacco. What do you think?'. At that point, a lively discussion begins. As you imagined, most of the committee members were not completely enthusiastic about ESG. Indeed, they were not convinced at all! You hear comments like: 'ESG is gobbledygook', 'Come on, that's completely nonsense', 'That's fine in Sweden, but here in Latin America, ESG will never work', 'Maybe in 20 years'. Many people speak at the same time. At some point, Mrs. López Guerrero stops the discussion: 'OK, that's enough. Incidentally, the new member of our committee did not speak. Would you please share us your viewpoint about ESG?'

Over to you!

2 Making finance ethical and inclusive

Contributors

Prof. Charles H. Cho, Schulich School of Business, York University Canada (ccho@schulich.yorku.ca).

Prof. Eduardo Henrique Diniz, FGV-EAESP (eduardo.diniz@fgv.br).

Prof. Antonio De Vito, IE Business School and Alma Mater University of Bologna (Antonio.De.vito@ie.edu).

Prof. Annelise Vendramini Felsberg, FGV-EAESP GVces (annelise. vendramini@fgv.br).

DOI: 10.4324/9781003317333-7

Financial and non-financial disclosure

As a future shareholder, would you pay? If so, how much more or less?

Charles H. Cho
Schulich School of Business, York University

You have put some savings away or come across a windfall. What's more, being practical-minded, instead of keeping it all under the mattress or depositing it in a low-interest savings account, you'd like to see this nest egg put to good use and hope to get a healthy return. Investment seems to be a perfect solution.

Fine, but then things become a little complex, not least because you're a conscious investor, aware of the harm business may cause to society and the planet, and determined to help transform it into doing good. In fact, you're one of the growing number of people who believe that sustainability matters are important, convinced that companies can and must actively bring light to the shadier side of the business of yesteryear. And, in order to do so, part of your plan to invest necessarily calls upon gathering information that will enable you to make the right, and *responsible*, investment decision.

From early shareholder studies that hark back to the 1970s and 1980s to recent studies in the 2000s (notably Chan & Milne, 1999; Holm & Rikhardsson, 2008; Liyanarachchi & Milne, 2005; Milne & Chan, 1999; Milne & Patten, 2002; Rikhardsson & Holm, 2008), interest in environmental disclosure for investment decisions has shifted dramatically from little or no interest to interested to expressly required, and even demanded.

In some countries, mostly emerging economies, local stock exchanges have created sustainability indexes catering for the lower liquidity of their markets to help investors have access to sustainability data at little or no cost.

But what of the developed economies and their investors? It is to be noted that the studies mentioned earlier have their shortcomings. Undertaken with participants from developed economies, those taking part were able to request any desired extra disclosure – financial or non-financial – at no additional cost. Moreover, the studies overlooked the trade-off dimension – to what extent investor-shareholders were ready to accept varying levels of financial and non-financial disclosure before making their decision. The

DOI: 10.4324/9781003317333-8

limits of these studies beg several questions: would future shareholders be willing to pay for more corporate financial, social, and environmental disclosure? Would they pay less for below-average disclosure? Would the interest of shareholders vary across industries? And would a firm's murky past of corporate misconduct incite shareholders to pay more for disclosure linked to that company?

A little bit of difference

Before tackling these questions, it might be a good idea to pause and reflect on the differences between financial and non-financial disclosure. Obviously, financial disclosure directly refers to financial consequences and has the advantage of being more tangible in nature – something that reassures shareholders in that the information is definite and objective. Moreover, a survey carried out in 2011 on retail shareholders revealed that they preferred hard economic financial facts over CSR-related information.

The difference with non-financial disclosure, on the other hand, lies in the fact that it covers information related more to potential risks and returns that can – or cannot – be translated into financial terms. As such, it assesses future financial prospects that are not wholly guaranteed. However, recent research has shown that additional CSR-related disclosure does have a positive impact on corporate financial performance, adding to the value of an organisation. Experiments conducted with shareholders too point towards non-financial disclosure swinging investment decisions.

In any case, be it financial or non-financial disclosure, firms that release more information seem to be more highly valued among investors and shareholders with a willingness to accept lower returns for companies providing full voluntary disclosures – very simply because more information for the shareholder enables better cash flow and risk forecasts to be made.

Put on your shareholder shoes

So how willing are shareholders to pay more for more information? Deploying the WTP concept – or *willing-to-pay* concept – based on a consumer model giving the price at which a customer would definitely purchase a product is useful. It gives a pertinent idea of the value shareholders and investors allocate to financial disclosure compared to social and environmental disclosure.

However, the *willing-to-pay* question must be gauged against previous research on non-financial disclosure. Firms working in environmentally sensitive sectors such as heavy industry or fossil fuel energy have been shown to be impacted most when providing information relating to their environmental performance. As such, the take is that shareholders will be interested in non-financial disclosure because it has more potential to influence financial returns.

Moreover, another claim is that shareholders' requests for non-financial information increase with firms that have, or have had, known issues linked to their social and environmental footprints. Financial managers are expected to deliver information on the measures and actions taken by the firm to improve effects on future cash flow and mitigate the level of risk linked to costly financial and reputational incidents.

Shareholders might also want to benchmark companies before their decision, requesting information across firms operating in the same sector in order to compare performance and, more importantly, compare risks. A telling example is that of investor scrutiny of BP in the wake of the Deepwater Horizon oil spill in the Gulf of Mexico in 2010.

Will they or won't they?

New research on the question of shareholders' willingness to pay focuses on 65 shareholders in New Zealand retail sector who were given a set of 12 choices each between two investment scenarios and varying degrees of financial and social and environmental disclosure and investment returns. The aim is to test the following hypotheses and identify which decisions shareholders made considering the costs involved in collecting more information on their investment targets. Moreover, what trade-offs do shareholders make?

- Shareholders are willing to pay more for more disclosure, or less for less disclosure.
- Shareholders put a greater value on obtaining more or less information on financial aspects than social and environmental aspects.
- The value they put on changes in disclosure varies across firms operating in different sectors.
- And finally, depending on whether a firm has a previous record of social and environmental misconduct, do shareholders give no value to obtaining more or less disclosure?

Let's take the findings one by one. Are investors willing to pay more for more disclosure? And what about the financial versus non-financial preference? Shareholders will indeed pay more for financial and environmental disclosure but seem hesitant – indeed unwilling – to pay for social disclosure. This *could* be due to the less 'close', less 'visible', and less tangible nature of social issues when compared to environmental issues.

This goes some way in establishing that investors are ready to lose out on returns in order to gain access to a higher number of corporate disclosures.

However, this preference shifts somewhat when the stakes are about moving from a below-average level of disclosure to an average level. Here, the shareholder views both financial and non-financial disclosure of equal value, which contrasts with former studies indicating that shareholders preferred financial to non-financial information.

When it comes to the value shareholders place on obtaining information for various companies operating in different sectors, findings gleaned from comparing mining versus sports clothing point to shareholders not rating disclosure differently.

And finally, do shareholders give no value to obtaining more or less disclosure if a firm has a previous record of social and environmental misconduct? Findings show no evidence to support this. Moreover, shareholders seem to be highly interested in receiving more than the minimum level of environmental disclosure, but less interested in obtaining above-average levels of either social or environmental disclosure.

These latest research findings can prove of interest to various stakeholders, including firms, in deciding on the level of disclosure required, as well as for regulators in assessing the need for financial disclosure regulation. Moreover, there may soon be a day when any type of additional disclosure may not cost the investor a cent – some stock markets and firms are now making integrated reporting a mandatory feature of disclosure to fulfil the need for (non-financial) transparency and in doing so add value to reputation, assets, and the firm.

Legal systems too play their part. Companies operating in regions where there is strong institutional presence and well-developed legal system that pushes firms to act more responsibly, also provide the framework and impetus for non-financial reporting to be offered for public scrutiny – not to mention shareholders and potential investors – free of charge. This can only be beneficial to the conscious investor and his savings. And beneficial too for the responsible firm.

Key takeaways

- Financial disclosure directly refers to financial consequences and has the advantage of being more tangible in nature. This reassures shareholders.
- Non-financial disclosure covers information related to potential risks and returns that can   or cannot – be translated into financial terms. It assesses future financial prospects that are not wholly guaranteed.
- CSR-related disclosure may have a positive impact on corporate financial performance, adding to the value of an organisation and it may swing shareholders' investment decisions.
- Firms that release more information are more highly valued among investors and shareholders who accept lower returns for companies

providing full voluntary disclosures – more information for the share-holder enables better cash flow and risk forecasts to be made.

• Recent research shows that shareholders will indeed pay more for financial and environmental disclosure but seem unwilling to pay for social disclosure.
• Shareholders seem to be highly interested in receiving more than the minimum level of environmental disclosure, but less interested in obtaining above-average levels of either social or environmental disclosure.
• There is a growing trend for stock markets and firms to resort to free, integrated reporting, publishing financial and non-financial information, and transparency that adds value to a firm's reputation, assets, and value.

Food for thought

• What about yourself as a potential shareholder? To what extent would you pay to receive more disclosure? And would you have a preference for financial or social and environmental information?
• Why would you, or not, buy shares in a petroleum company?
• To what extent does the publishing of non-financial information amount to greenwashing? How can this information be trusted or verified?

References

Chan, C. and Milne, M. (1999) Investor reactions to corporate environmental saints and sinners: an experimental analysis, *Accounting and Business Research*, vol. 29, no. 4, 265–279.

Holm, C. and Rikhardsson, P. (2008) Experienced and novice investors: does environmental information influence investment allocation decisions?, *European Accounting Review*, vol. 17, no. 3, 537–557.

Liyanarachchi, G. and Milne, M. (2005) Comparing the investment decisions of accounting practitioners and students: an empirical study on hte adequacy of student surrogates, *Accounting Forum*, vol. 2, no. 3, 121–135.

Milne, M and Chan, C. (1999) Narrative corporate social disclosures: how much of a difference do they make to investment decision-making? *British Accounting Review*, 31, 439–457.

Milne, M. and Patten, D. (2002) Securing organizational legitimacy: an experimental decision case examining the impact of environmental disclosures, *Accounting, Auditing & Accountability Journal*, vol. 15, no. 3, 372–405.

Rikhardsson, P. and Holm, C. (2008) The effect of environmental information on investment allocation decisions-an experimental study, *Business Strategy and the Environment*, vol. 17, no. 6, 382–397.

Related research: Are Shareholders Willing to Pay for Financial, Social and Environmental Disclosure? A Choice-based Experiment, June 2021, European Accounting Review, DOI: 10.1080/09638180.2021.1944890

The journey from community bank to solidarity fintech through digital social currency

Eduardo Henrique Diniz
FGV-EAESP

Hard times

Brazil is a beautiful and wicked paradox. Home to some of the world's finest educational and research institutions, rich in resources, agriculture, and industries, frequently hailed in the 1970s to the 1990s as the 21st-century economic giant to be reckoned with – only to slip back before the tipping point – and renown throughout the world for its vibrant and innovative arts and sports. And yet, despite all this, 50 million people in Brazil now live below the poverty line. Wounded by the explosion in foreign debt that harks back to the 1980s, the fragile banking system has been riding the storm of volatile interest rates and inflation – causing banks to seek shelter in safer and more profitable segments of the population.

This has meant a widening of the divide between those able to access traditional banking services and those left behind – namely a large majority of young adults, the less educated, and those working in the shadow economy.

Paradoxically too, this has given rise to another of Brazil's beautiful innovations – that of solidarity finance. One of its flagbearers is Palmas e-Dinheiro, a Solidarity Fintech owned by Banco Palmas.

From paper to digital

A digital venture, e-Dinheiro has a purpose and vision that is characterised by its commitment to financial inclusion, a belief that local is beautiful in the guise of local economic development, and its traditional, strong identification with Brazil's community banking movement.

The roots of this community banking movement are with Banco Palmas and stretch back to the late 1990s when residents of a poor neighbourhood district in the suburbs of Fortaleza in Ceará state began a research project to attempt to understand how their local economy worked and why they remained among the poorer off. The results showed that a large part of

DOI: 10.4324/9781003317333-9

inhabitants' income was actually spent outside the neighbourhood – and so the initiative was born to encourage local consumption to boost local economy through a community bank, the Banco Palmas.

The bank provided local folks with the possibility to access credit through a small, paper card called the PalmaCard. And as this became increasingly popular, it became apparent that some form of more effective liquidity tool was required to deal with this scaling up of operations. Accordingly, in 2001, Banco Palmas launched a paper-format community currency. But what was initially designed as a local currency grew as a model for other communities across Brazil, so that by 2018, the parent association, Instituto Palmas, was able to provide BRL14m (about USD3m) in microcredit to thousands of entrepreneurs – most of them were women who had until then been denied access to the financial system.

The expansion of Banco Palmas – from a few hundred to several thousands of clients and the model for nearly 100 such banks springing up throughout Brazil – also brought with it its problems. Most notably, that of high costs related to printing, managing, and issuing a physical paper currency. How to overcome this? Going digital seemed the answer. Already in use in emerging economies in Africa and Asia, digital currency based on mobile payment systems has offered the possibility to scale up operations and lower costs – and in doing so spark off greater local economic development.

The subsequent development in 2012 of the first mobile payment platform brought with it a sore experience and many lessons. These were drawn not only from the classic challenges faced by for-profit enterprises at the pivotal moment of scaling up but also from the disruption caused by the transition to a provider of digital services, as well as the threat posed to sense purpose and founding values.

First attempt: partners, target audience, context, and . . . failure

In Brazil, in the early 2010s, the only way to issue a mobile payment system was to partner with traditional companies working within the telecom and financial sectors. Launching the digital payment project in 2012, working approaches and working culture inevitably came to clash, with Banco Palmas executives feeling excluded from decision-making – ideas either being disapproved of or too time-consuming. The relationship also suffered from lack of coordination among various partners.

An additional challenge was that of Banco Palmas' client base. Through the paper currency format, and traditionally mostly women entrepreneurs accessing first-time microcredit, the switch to digital operations posed the threat of excluding certain beneficiaries. Either clients could not access the service due to a lack of electricity supply or internet connection, or because some base-of-the-pyramid clients lacked the tech skills and confidence in mobile payments.

Added to that was a shift in context, 2013 marking the year when Brazil's political and economic mood began to change. Notably, it was the Federal Government's perception of its role in the solidarity economy that manifested itself in the National Secretary of the Solidarity Economy (SNAES) gradually losing its influence and impact to develop public policy.

Despite the huge potential of the initiative, Banco Palmas' initial experiment with mobile payment was unsuccessful. Operational difficulties, withdrawal of government support and endorsement, and conflicts of interest and opposing expectations among partners being the main factors responsible for the project's failure.

However, later in 2013, positive news came in the form of new regulations on digital payment platforms coming into vigour and issued by the Central Bank. Although clauses specific to the solidarity economy were not explicitly included, these new regulations enabled non-profit organisations to offer a broader range of financial services and develop their digital payment platforms without the need to partner with the traditional financial and telecom players. And as the new bill took effect, Instituto Palmas of which Banco Palmas was a part found itself with newly gained autonomy and bearing a new identity – that of solidarity fintech.

Second attempt: solidarity fintech

In 2015, Instituto Palmas made a second attempt to launch an online inclusive banking initiative, partnering with MoneyClip, a startup Brazilian company specialising in developing digital platforms for financial inclusion. The product – the e-Dinheiro – enabled community banks to offer payment services via SMS, mobile apps, and the internet.

Despite the repeat of former challenges posed by entering into partnership, the Instituto Palmas and MoneyClip were able to avoid the deeper-rooted problems associated with the first attempt to create a digital offer. A major difference this time was that Instituto Palmas retained more control over the digital platform, thereby ensuring that the design and roll-out of the tool kept its bottom-up roots in order to cater for the specific needs of its customer base.

However, fintech poses inherent issues regardless of the nature of the player. Once again, scaling up posed a major challenge. Quite apart from the necessary need for additional human, capital, and investment resources, the shift into bigger operations meant setting up tighter processes and project management methods that included KPIs, all of which required a wider skill set. On the Palmas side, governance too posed a challenge – how to continue to work with its inherent solidarity purpose, values, and identity intact while becoming a fintech provider and maintaining control over decision-making on the platform.

Shortly after its successful launch, e-Dinheiro was adopted by the network of community banks, and by 2018, 81 such banks were registered on the platform, the majority aimed at their local communities. In some cases, it spelt success – one of them was the Banco Mumbuca with thousands of users benefitting from local government endorsement to offer a conditional cash transfer programme to its clients. It is in the example of Banco Mumbuca that the potential for the e-Dinheiro is most prominently demonstrated. And also that of the journey from solidarity bank to fintech provider.

Adoption by the solidarity banking community and wider impact

Founded in 2013 in the city of Maricá, Banco Mumbuca had operated a POS – point-of-sale – debit card system. Their activity gathered together a large network of stakeholders: its client base of 12,000 families in the city at the time of the launching, local community staff, the Instituto Palmas responsible for training Banco Mumbuca staff, the city government, local businesses, other residents of the city who are also able to use the new tool, and finally, the POS card technology providers. While successful – the POS system driving sizable amounts of money into the local economy – it was also limited in that it was tied and governed by an agreement with the local government.

The opening up of regulations and the belief that the future of solidarity banking was digital, led to the POS card providers being fully replaced by the Banco Mumbuca staff in 2018, that together with the e-Dinheiro platform took control over all the operation of benefit payments disbursement in the city. Although the maintenance of the payments was based on cards, especially among the elders and less digitally literate population, it soon became evident that the new digital and online system presented a number of advantages. Not only did it reduce costs relating to the manufacturing, distribution, and management of plastic debit cards, the mobile platform also allowed customers to access an increased number of services such as checking accounts for the payment of bills, savings accounts, peer-to-peer transfers, and micro-loans for mobile phone purchase. In addition, and in keeping with its solidarity economy values, e-Dinheiro followed a policy of making 'mumbucas' (its virtual money) circulate as a real currency within the city. Moreover, by charging merchants with lower fees than what those of credit card companies, Banco Mumbuca raised funds to begin micro-credit ops.

Proximity with its local customer base too proved advantageous in that features and services were able to be continuously updated or launched, tailored to the particular requirements of the region and its populations.

The notion of solidarity was kept intact. Palmas e-Dinheiro both effectively reinvested in each community and improved the human capital and physical assets of the community banks from revenues earned through its online platform. As such, and set aside as a truly social fintech, the Palmas e-Dinheiro can boast of achieving the highest social impact possible.

But it was the COVID-19 pandemic of 2020–2021 that also saw the powerful potential of the e-Dinheiro digital currency – the mumbuca – take off. Initially created for the unbanked, the digital format of the e-Dinheiro meant that it was a digital solution accessible by anyone. Indeed, in an attempt to cater for micro-entrepreneurs who found themselves without income due to the effects of the pandemic, the city offered an emergency basic income in the form of a salary paid in mumbucas via the e-Dinheiro app. At the height of the pandemic, e-Dinheiro reached nearly half of the city's population – some 80,000 people.

Far from being a paradox, the transformation of the Palmas currency into the e-Dinheiro mobile payment platform goes far in providing impactful solutions to the wicked problems that Brazil faces. Some may say that it indeed deserves a place among the country's other beautiful innovations.

Key takeaways

- Brazil has been in the vanguard of solidarity finance and community banking services since the 1990s, partly as an alternative solution to counter traditional banks' low-risk approach in targeting 'wealthier' client bases.
- More than 50 million people in Brazil now live below the poverty line, making it difficult or impossible for young people, women entrepreneurs, the less educated, and informal economy workers to access banking services.
- The Banco Palmas is a successful example of community banking, initially providing the means for local communities to access credit through a paper card called the PalmaCard. In 2001, it launched a paper-format community currency. By 2018, the parent association, Instituto Palmas, was able to provide BRL14m (about USD3m) in microcredit to thousands of entrepreneurs.
  Typical clients include women, the young, the less educated, and those working in the informal economy.

- The first attempt to Palmas digitalisation in 2012 met with failure due to differences in culture, operating approaches, conflicting goals and interests, and decision-making processes with traditional telecoms and financial partners.
- Bottom-of-the-pyramid clients were also not yet ready to adopt digital solutions due to lack of electricity supply, internet connection, and skills and confidence in new technology.
- Change in government regulations in 2013 offered the possibility for non-banking institutions to provide payment systems.
- A second attempt in 2015 with start-up MoneyClip met with success, despite challenges due to the transition to digital, scaling up, new skills requirements, and Instituto Palmas keeping control over decision-making.
- Shortly after its launch, e-Dinheiro was adopted by the network of community banks, including Banco Mumbuca which added this platform to its plastic debit cards operations to deliver social benefits to the poor in the city of Maricá.
- Although some less literate users still kept using the card system, the expansion of the e-Dinheiro platform reduced costs, widened its services offer, and enabled lower fees to merchants that accept payments in mumbucas to fund microcredit in the city.
- Proximity with customers enables tailor-made services and innovations for local communities.
- The COVID pandemic saw the digital currency being offered as a minimum salary to cover micro-entrepreneurs who have lost their revenue streams.
- Also available to the wider population, at the height of the pandemic, the currency was used by 80,000 people in the city of Maricá, almost half the city's population.

Food for thought

- What examples of Tech4Good can you see in your country?
- To what extent is technology an answer to building an inclusive society? In what sectors can it do this? And what sectors and populations will suffer damage as a result of digital technology?
- If you were to create a tech start-up with the aim of helping people and the planet, what product or service would you offer? What would make it unique? What problems would it solve and what needs would it satisfy?

Related work and research: Innovations in Social Finance, From Community Bank to Solidarity Fintech: The Case of Palmas e-Dinheiro in Brazil, 2021, Springer

Micro case study 3: Finance

After much discussion, the board of the NAIRDA bank decided to implement a broad revision of its investment policy, in order to include ESG considerations. The bank has a large, diversified investment portfolio, ranging across many industries, and with large stakes in many of the most important companies in Latin America. The following is an excerpt from a discussion in the bank's investment committee:

Mr. Irrigarabia, Investment Director: This ESG is nice, we agree on principle. But in practice, how to choose this or that share based on ESG? We do not have much information about ESG issues in the region, and international ESG rating agencies rarely cover companies in the region.

Mr. Bianchi, Senior Analyst: Well, some companies provide sustainability reports. Indeed, some companies have been continuously publishing some reports, in many cases following international guidelines.

Mr. Irrigarabia: Come on, that's just tick-the-box stuff. I read some of those reports, they all look the same. I would bet that the same consultants made them.

Mrs. López Guerrero, Committee President: On the other hand, there are, of course, the sustainability indexes. For instance, the Brazilian stock exchange launched its sustainability index more than 15 years ago. And several of them have been launched in the last years in the region. We could just take a look at the compositions of those indexes. I mean, any company that enters such an index is *a priori* a step ahead.

Mr. Bianchi: Good idea! But we need to be careful with the method.

Mr. Irrigarabia: Why?

Mr. Bianchi: Because, depending on the method the index uses, one could find controversial firms. For instance, if the index uses a 'best-in-class' approach, it means that the best company in each sector will be chosen, even if that sector remains controversial.

Mrs. López Guerrero: You have a point. Let's cast a glance at the composition of this sustainability index. Look, there's an oil company!

Mr. Irrigarabia: That's very debatable, I admit. At the same time, the rationale for a firm in a controversial sector remaining in a 'best-in-class' index is that the index creates a competition for improving ESG issues in such a sector.

Mrs. Schmidt, Senior Analyst: Not sure that argument will fly with our younger investors. For them, keeping an oil company in our portfolio is a no-no. And any explanation we put forward could be perceived as a mere justification.

Mrs. López Guerrero: OK, let's summarise. We want to implement ESG in all our investment portfolios. The problem is that we do not have much information on the region. Some companies, but not all of them, publish sustainability reports. Besides, international ESG rating agencies cover a few companies, but that is more of the exception than the rule. And we have these sustainability indexes. We need to prepare a formal ESG investment policy for the coming years. We need to provide assurance to our clients that we take ESG seriously and that we use the best available information to support our choices.

How would you state that investment policy, taking into consideration the context and the limitations to access ESG information?

A global minimum tax

An end to the multinationals 'racing to the bottom'?

Antonio De Vito
IE Business School and Alma Mater University of Bologna

Companies, much like people, are always looking for a good deal. With globalisation and the increasing trend for enterprises to set up operations abroad and tap into unchartered markets, the opportunities to boost revenues through their products and services have never been more readily reachable. Opportunities too have come in the form of tax avoidance – or put more euphemistically, tax optimisation.

With subsidiaries abroad, companies are bound by both their home and host-country tax systems. Current international tax laws offer these enterprises a choice – either pay tax in the home country, the host country, or both. The largest MNCs that include some of the world's most popular brands and services have for some years benefitted from this. Subsidiaries set up in an overseas location pay only taxes from profits earned within its borders, whereas the home country activities have a choice – either top up the overseas tax with its own or exempt this from further taxation. This depends on whether the home country exercises a worldwide or territorial tax system.

As such, if a home country uses a worldwide tax system approach, its home tax rates apply to both the home and overseas subsidiaries' profits while benefitting from foreign tax credits to soften up the taxation of foreign profits. In practice, the MNC initially pays a corporate tax on its foreign income earned abroad. Once the foreign subsidiary passes on its profits to the parent company, the home country then charges the gross accumulated profit using its statutory corporate tax rate.

The MNC's foreign subsidiaries, however, can set their own advantageous local tax rates in order to cushion the blow. And if the home country – let's take the USA – puts off taxing the MNC until its overseas income is collected, the overall tax charge can be substantially lower. Indeed, the US tax system long exempted overseas profits that were considered permanently invested abroad. This explains why American MNCs – Amazon

DOI: 10.4324/9781003317333-10

and Google being most under the spotlight among them – have managed to accumulate a massive $2.6 trillion in capital that avoids the taxman.

A knock-on effect has been that, in an attempt to attract foreign companies to set up, host countries have tended to lower their tax rates to the lowest possible, thereby creating a 'race to the bottom'. Home countries therefore lose out, with MNCs relocating jobs, expertise, assets, and ultimately tax revenues which governments could sorely use for financing education, health, its armed forces, and national infrastructure.

One step beyond

The shifting of profits from high-tax to low-tax countries abroad is nothing new. As long ago as 2013, the OECD began tackling the problem, launching a project to prevent such movement that was calculated to amount to 10% of the world's corporate tax revenue – an estimated USD240 billion. Baptised the BEPS (Base Erosion and Profit Shifting) project, little progress was made until the OECD decided to go a step further with the deeper, broader Global Anti-Base Erosion (GloBE) Proposal that included a new and key clement in the idea of reaching consensus over a global minimum tax.

The idea, based upon President Joe Biden's proposal of setting a 21% rate, depended on whether a multinational's home country chose to operate a worldwide or territorial tax system. If worldwide, an MNC would continue to pay the statutory corporate tax rate on worldwide income and retain foreign tax credit for the taxes it pays in the host country. However, the host country would face a levy on its rate to bring it up to the 21% mark. Moreover, this would not pose a threat to attract inward foreign investment and could, potentially, prevent the 'race to the bottom' from occurring.

A second scenario is whether the multinational's home country chooses to adopt a territorial tax system – meaning no tax on foreign profits and no tax credit for the MNC. In this situation, the top-up (levy) to 21% imposed on the host country would represent the only additional taxes to be paid in the home country.

Would the GloBE proposal sign the end of tax avoidance and profit shifting? Most certainly yes, if the one thing that induces MNCs to shift tax is removed – the tax differential between home and host countries – and tax revenues in high-tax countries would be expected to increase. One could also argue that an easier solution would be for home countries to move directly to a worldwide tax system rather than adopt a global minimum tax. But this wouldn't spell an end to host countries in emerging countries to continue to offer generous packages that include lower taxes in an attempt to lure wealth and jobs to their economies.

In the year 2021–2023

At the end of 2021, the OECD announced that a deal had been struck between 137 countries to introduce a global minimum tax for MNCs that saw the previous proposed rate of 21% drop to 15%. This effectively added a second pillar to the former BEPS and GloBE projects and is intended to come into force in 2023 for multinationals earning revenue of more than USD820 million per annum. The OECD estimates that this measure will generate roughly USD150 billion per year in additional corporate taxes worldwide – manna from heaven for all those social, health, and educational needs mentioned previously. Of those additional corporate tax revenues, Barake, Neef, Chouc, and Zucman (2021) estimate that the European Union stands to gain the most (i.e. about a quarter of what it currently collects), whereas the United States would raise about USD57 billion yearly.

Yes, but . . .

However, these estimates are based on the assumption that there is no reduction in the tax base upon which the global minimum tax applies (i.e. the so-called 'carve-outs'). Indeed, a side effect of the global minimum tax could also be that host countries compete with tax base instruments to attract real foreign direct investments/firms in an attempt to offset the revenue loss from less profit shifting.

The danger of offsetting tax incentives appears to be real. Switzerland, for example, is already considering offering tax subsidies, such as research grants, social security deductions, and tax credits, to firms relocating within its borders to compensate for the revenue loss from less cross-border profit shifting.* If such policy responses were to be followed by other countries, the global minimum tax may not achieve its intended effect, and the deal signed in December 2021 would have to be complemented with restrictions that limit competition with other tax tools in order to raise the envisioned revenue gains.

Such restrictions would not even be entirely new. Take the European Union as an example. The regulations on state aids already prevent member countries from favouring certain firms through tax subsidies at the expense of their competitors. Following the EU framework, one could therefore argue that such restrictions may have to be agreed upon and enforced at the worldwide level in order for the global minimum to be truly effective. In sum, the global minimum creates opportunities but poses also challenges for countries. Whether revenue gains from the global minimum tax will be as large as countries are hoping for is yet to be seen.

www.swissinfo.ch/eng/switzerland-plans-subsidies-to-offset-g7-corporate-tax-plan/46696800

Key takeaways

- Globalisation and the increasing trend for enterprises to set up operations abroad have led to cases of tax avoidance or tax optimisation. US MNCs have managed to accumulate an estimated $2.6 trillion in capital that avoids the taxman.
- Current international tax laws offer these enterprises a choice – either pay tax in the home country, the host country, or both.
- If a home country uses a worldwide tax system approach, its home tax rates apply to both the home and overseas subsidiaries' profits while benefitting from foreign tax credits to soften up the taxation of foreign profits.
- The MNC's foreign subsidiaries, however, can set their own advantageous local tax rates in order to cushion the blow.
- The USA puts off taxing the MNC until its overseas income is collected. The overall tax charge can be substantially lower because the US exempts overseas profits that were considered permanently invested abroad.
- In 2013, the OECD launched the BEPS (Base Erosion and Profit Shifting) project, and then the Global Anti-Base Erosion (GloBE) Proposal that included the idea of a global minimum tax.
- In 2021, the OECD announced that a deal had been struck between 137 countries to introduce a global minimum tax for MNCs of 15%, intended to come into force in 2023 for multinationals earning revenue of more than USD820 million per annum.
- But the global minimum creates opportunities but poses also challenges for countries.
- A side effect of the global minimum tax could also be that host countries compete with tax base instruments to attract real foreign direct investments/firms in an attempt to offset the revenue loss from less profit shifting.

Food for thought

- To what extent do you think companies are right to attempt to minimise their tax payments? Why or why not? And who benefits?
- Imagine that you wish to start up a company. What types of corporate taxes and charges exist? How worthwhile do you think it is to create your company in your country? And if you believe the conditions aren't right, where would you envisage setting up instead? Why?

- How do you see the global minimum tax system working out? If you were working for your finance ministry of your country, what would you use this additional cash flow for?
- And, in reality, to what extent do you think governments would put this tax to good use?

Reference

Barake, M., Neef, T., Chouc, P., Zucman, G. (2021) Revenue effects of the global minimum tax, *Eutax Observatory*, accessed online at: www.taxobservatory.eu, December 2022.

Can Bitcoin be subject to an ESG analysis?

Annelise Vendramini Felsberg

FGV-EAESP Center for Sustainability Studies (FGVces)

Bitcoin meets ESG analysis

As a medium of exchange, unit of account, and a store of value, money facilitates almost all human endeavours. From the time the first coins ever were found in the Temple of Artemis in Turkey, dating back to 600 BC, to the present-day US Dollar bills, societies all over the world and throughout the ages have worked hard to make money available, portable, and reliable. Economics and Finance, as disciplines, have thrived in the last 200 years to help individuals, organisations, and societies to overcome their capital allocation problems and eventually reach their ultimate objectives, with innovation at the centre of this process.

With the launch of Bitcoin in 2009, crypto assets were an important addition to a long list of innovations in monetary systems and in the investment universe. Bitcoin's origins go back to 2008, when a programmer going under the pseudonym of Satoshi Nakamoto published a paper under the title *A Peer-to-Peer Electronic Cash System*. Both a crypto asset and a peer-to-peer electronic payment system based on cryptographic proof instead of trust, Bitcoin is considered an alternative way for people to make transactions without resorting to a trusted third party such as a bank. To remain secure, ensure viability, and avoid duplication, Bitcoin relies on an encryption system – the Blockchain – which registers all the operations and transactions within its network. Since its launch, other crypto assets have followed – Ethereum and Tether, among them – although Bitcoin remains the most traded crypto asset with over 40% share of the market.

Another innovation in the investment universe is the sustainable investment approach which consists of adding to the traditional investment analysis environmental (E), social (S), and governance (G) considerations in asset selection and portfolio management through an ESG analysis. According to this perspective, ESG – Environmental, Social, and Governance – factors are important for investors because, although non-financial, they can

DOI: 10.4324/9781003317333-11

be used to identify risks, volatility, and the potentiality of long-term growth and therefore return on investment while at the same time recognising that investments have impacts on society and on the environment. The Global Sustainable Investment Review estimates that there is at least one aspect of ESG in nearly 40% of all assets under management.

Two recent innovations in finance – the increased interest in Bitcoin as a financial asset and the growth of the sustainable investment approach and ESG analysis – lead to the question of whether the Bitcoin can be subject to evaluation through an ESG analysis.

ESG strategies and Bitcoin

There are at least five strategies associated with ESG analysis: negative screening, positive screening and best-in-class, shareholder engagement, thematic investment, and ESG integration. The negative screening strategy excludes from portfolios certain sectors, themes, or issues deemed not investable due to social, environmental, or governance reasons. The positive screening and best-in-class approaches do not exclude any sectors, themes, or issues *a priori* but seek the best among industry peers (best-in-class) or include only assets whose ESG performance is above a certain threshold (positive screening). Shareholder engagement seeks to influence corporate behaviour to improve its ESG performance. The thematic investment strategy actively seeks investments in assets in certain themes, sectors, and companies that explicitly contribute to solutions to sustainability matters, such as renewable energy or waste treatment. ESG integration is the integration of ESG factors in traditional financial analysis, such as valuation and multiples analysis. The sustainable investor adopts one or several of these strategies to mitigate ESG risks, usually related to financial products such as equities, corporate and sovereign debts, and real assets. It is uncommon to perform an ESG analysis on currencies – the dollar, pound sterling, or euro, for example – or payment systems. As a decentralised system, subjecting Bitcoin to an ESG analysis would have no practical effects if the sustainable investor adopts shareholder engagement and ESG integration strategies, for example. However, other strategies such as negative, positive screening, or thematic investment allow some consideration about the ESG aspects of Bitcoin.

The E in ESG

The E in ESG relates to the relationship that a business has with the natural environment and takes into consideration aspects such as renewable and non-renewable energy used in its activities. Undoubtedly, one key feature that comes under scrutiny during the E analysis is Bitcoin mining, the process of solving complex mathematical problems necessary to maintain the public ledger of transactions. Also, as a result, new Bitcoins are created.

Mining requires massive amounts of electricity. According to the International Energy Agency, in 2020, 63% of total world gross electricity production came from fossil fuels. Any activity highly dependent on electricity has an important contribution to the global carbon footprint.

In addition, mining requires highly specialised machines with great computing power which becomes obsolete every three years, maybe fewer in the future. Faced with the dilemma of the productivity/time ratio that faces traditional industries, crypto asset miners have resorted to replacing equipment before the effective life-cycle end of their computers – thus raising the issue of electronic waste and recycling. Also, the high turnover of equipment increases the demand for more raw materials, putting pressure on extractive activities that explore natural resources such as minerals.

SG – the social and governance dimensions to Bitcoin

In an ESG analysis, social aspects cover all of those aspects relating to the business impact on human life. Internally in terms of working conditions and human resources practices, as well as the business's effect on its suppliers and even wider stakeholders such as local communities and regions in which the firm operates. Governance aspects are the processes and structures that help shareholders to oversee the business and management of a company. Governance is a dimension that involves analysing and influencing decision-makers: in a decentralised system such as Bitcoin, this is a pointless attempt. Nevertheless, the fact that Bitcoin is decentralised is a feature that might be considered in the governance dimension of an ESG analysis.

One special concern regarding Bitcoin is the risks linked to the legality of the uses it enables. Innovated to ensure decentralised transactions and grant anonymity in certain circumstances, Bitcoin can be used to bypass the law. As such, Bitcoin can facilitate ecological crimes, activities that violate human rights, fraud, money laundering, corruption, and even terrorism. Bitcoin users tend to prioritise privacy over safety and for users of the conventional financial system, safety over privacy. Investor security is also an important issue with Bitcoin, because trading platforms and wallet providers have been hacked leading to huge losses for investors.

From the conventional finance perspective, governments have attempted to harness, or at least provide guiding frameworks, which are designed to manage social and environmental risks. Deposits in a financial institution under the supervision of Brazil's Central Bank (the BCB), for example, are used to provide loans and finance legal entities under applicable social and environmental risk laws and regulations. The same does not apply to Bitcoin. Interestingly, Blockchain, the technology on which Bitcoin is based, is currently being used to enhance traceability and verification in a whole variety of areas – from writing up and protecting health records to food security and voting systems. This is independent of its use for crypto assets.

Is Bitcoin suitable?

Suitability refers to the requirement that an investment strategy respects the investment objectives and the risk profile of the investor. Crypto assets are by nature volatile and as such, potential investors in Bitcoin necessarily need to have an appetite for risk.

Some have accused Bitcoin of being a Ponzi scheme – a form of financial fraud that pays off earlier investors with money invested from recent investors. Several big names have spoken out against Bitcoin. Charlie Munger, the investor and businessman, has likened the Bitcoin to a poison. Nassim Taleb, the statistician and risk analyst expert, has also criticised Bitcoin and called into question its claims of being without government and a reliable bringer of value – either in the short or the long term. Given this, it must also be said that investors with pure speculative interest are not limited to crypto assets – they have always existed, even in conventional financial products.

Table 1 summarises the ESG aspects of Bitcoin discussed in this insight.

Table 1 Summary of ESG aspects applicable to Bitcoin.

Aspects regarding ESG analysis and Bitcoin	Description	Examples
Bitcoin is a crypto asset and a decentralised payment system.	ESG analyses are usually performed on equities, corporate and sovereign debts, and real estate.	It is uncommon to perform ESG analysis on other assets such as currencies (the US dollar or euro, for example) or on a system, such as the whole 'banking system'.

(Continued)

Table 1 (Continued)

Aspects regarding ESG analysis and Bitcoin	Description	Examples
There is not a single ESG approach: there are at least five ESG strategies.	Two ESG strategies such as shareholder engagement and ESG integration are not applicable to Bitcoin. Negative screening, positive screening and best-in-class, and thematic investment allow ESG consideration for Bitcoin.	**Shareholder engagement:** not applicable because Bitcoin is a decentralised system, so there is not a group of decision-makers to be influenced towards better ESG practices. **ESG Integration**: not applicable to integrate ESG aspects in valuation and multiples analysis for Bitcoin. **Negative screening**: Sustainable investors might exclude Bitcoin from the investable universe because it enables shady activities, and is heavy on electricity usage, use of materials, and waste generation. **Positive screening/best-in-class**: Sustainable investors can compare Bitcoin with other crypto assets and decide which has the best ESG performance against a set of pre-defined parameters. **Thematic investment**: Sustainable investors might consider investing in Bitcoin to help advance its underlying technology (Blockchain) which can enhance trust, transparency, and effectiveness in a whole variety of areas.

Aspects regarding ESG analysis and Bitcoin	Description	Examples
Environmental aspects worth considering.	These are related to the impact of Bitcoin mining on the natural environment.	High electricity consumption which comes primarily from fossil fuels leads to high carbon footprint. High use of materials and electronic waste generation due to obsolescence of equipment used for mining.
Social and governance aspects are worth considering.	Social – impact on society. Governance – aspects that help shareholders to oversee the business and management of a company.	Bitcoin can enable activities that bypass the law, such as ecological crimes, activities that violate human rights, fraud, money laundering, corruption, and even terrorism. Suitability of investments in Bitcoin to investor risk profile. Investor security is key because trading platforms and wallet providers have been hacked leading to huge losses to investors. Governance: in such a decentralised system there is not a group of decision-makers to be influenced. Nevertheless, the fact that Bitcoin is decentralised is a feature that might be considered in the governance dimension of an ESG analysis.

Key takeaways

- Launched in 2009, Bitcoin is a crypto asset that works on the principle of providing anonymity under certain circumstances. It can prove attractive for potential investors.
- ESG – Environmental, Social, and Governance – factors are important for investors to identify risks, volatility, and the potentiality of long-term growth and return on investment. Also for the sustainable investor with an interest in either helping to improve business, society, and the planet or excluding controversial industries.
- ESG analysis of Bitcoin brings light on mining activities and the intensive use of electricity leading to a high carbon footprint.
- The rapid renewal of materials and hardware with an aim to remain efficient also calls into question Bitcoin's carbon footprint and its impact on the natural environment.
- On the social and governance dimensions, Bitcoin presents the following risks: it may attract illegal usage in the form of transactions concerning money laundering, corruption, and terrorism. It can cover the dilemma an investor has to face between privacy and safety.
- The technology Bitcoin uses – Blockchain – can be considered positive in terms of ESG, being currently used for increasing traceability and verification of activities such as health records, food security, and secure voting, among others.
- The volatile nature of Bitcoin raises questions about investor suitability (the ethical, legal standard of a product offered to an investor).

Food for thought

- To what extent would you invest in Bitcoin or another crypto asset? Why or why not?
- Think of three ways Bitcoin technology – Blockchain – could be put to further good and responsible use for business, society, and the planet.
- In what ways do you think Bitcoin and others are revolutionary? What do you think of its future?

The dilemma of the 'microfinance graduate'

The missing middle

Savita Shankar
University of Pennsylvania

Many developing countries have placed special importance on financial inclusion in their policy agendas in recent times. An inclusive financial system implies the availability of a continuity of financial services for all income groups offering a range of financial services with no gaps in provision. It is here that microfinance kicks in and where better to focus than the birthplace of microfinance – Asia, or more specifically Pakistan, Bangladesh, and India. Indeed, the Micro Finance Institutes (MFIs) in these countries have been the cornerstone in providing financial access and supporting myriad promising local businesses and brands.

However, these countries also face a common problem: there is a gap in the financial system that fails to address the needs of MFI borrowers who outgrow microfinance and require larger loans that are not as large as the needs of Small and Medium Enterprises (SMEs). These borrowers are referred to as *MFI graduates* and the gap – *the missing middle*.

Effective, moderate, and ineffective borrowers

It is not common for all MFI borrowers to become MFI graduates. A study in India revealed three possible outcomes when an individual gains access to microfinance. The first is effective MFI borrowers who utilise their loans to generate sufficient margins after payment of principal and interest. These are the MFI graduates or effective utilisers.

The second category are borrowers who use their loans for business activity too but do not receive sufficient margins and hence do not see rapid increases in income due to microcredit. These borrowers are referred to as cash flow smoothers since they primarily use the loans to smoothen cash flow and manage the day-to-day operations.

And the final category of borrowers uses the majority of their loans for non-business purposes (such as repayment of existing loans or consumption

DOI: 10.4324/9781003317333-12

expenditures). Individuals in this category usually find it hard to service the loan and eventually default or drop out. Such individuals are categorised as ineffective utilisers.

Let's focus on the effective utilisers – the *Graduates*. In India, an estimated 15% to 20% of all MFI borrowers fall under this category.

India and the missing middle

Financial exclusion is a critical problem in India. According to the World Bank's Global Findex database, in 2014, only 56.3% of individuals above the age of 25 had an account and only 8.8% had a formal borrowing account. For a country with a population of over one billion people, that's a lot of people with no access to financial institutions and support.

Microfinance in the country hinges on two main players: self-help groups and MFIs. The former model was originally promoted by the National Bank for Agriculture and Rural Development, while MFIs were promoted principally by individual entrepreneurs.

The missing middle is also apparent in the Indian microfinance system. The upper limit of microfinance loans being 100,000 INR (approximately USD1,300) and the lower limit for SME financing by commercial banks being around 1,000,000 INR (USD13,000), there is a considerable gap between the two client segments. This means that successful micro-entrepreneurs who wish to scale up and need extra funding to do it are faced with the missing middle – too big to take advantage of a micro-loan and too small to benefit from a medium-sized loan.

As a result of this gap, many entrepreneurs depend on informal sources of financing, including family and friends. The problem is that the latter usually have a limited pool of funds. Where to turn to? Moneylenders and chit funds – but these operators often charge very high-interest rates. A dilemma indeed.

Financing options for MFI graduates in India

The biggest barrier to banks in catering to the MFI graduate segment is the high-cost nature of their operations. Even though there is a provision for banks to use direct sales agents to reduce costs, reaching a satisfactory arrangement for both parties is often challenging. Moreover, since catering to the missing middle typically involves a considerable investment of employee time, it is often unviable given the small size of the loan.

MFIs can be potential lenders to MFI graduates but the main challenge here is to develop the ability to carry out a detailed credit appraisal. For this, MFIs would need to have training programmes for their large number of field officers. Another challenge is the availability of funding, as providing larger loans would require them to access a larger volume of funds.

NBFCs – or non-banking financial companies – cater to niche segments through a dense network of branches with credit officers who are responsible for the entire transaction from identifying customers to the collection of money. However, as the missing middle is highly diverse, other niche segments need to be identified and specific NBFCs are created to cater for them.

In India, rural banks, serving all companies in rural areas, struggle with low repayment rates. In order to address this problem, many of those banks have a dedicated staff for identifying potential borrowers.

Government initiatives to help fill the gap

The Indian government has indeed acknowledged the missing middle and its MFI graduates, seeing a source of employment generation. Several recent policy initiatives have seen the day to address this segment.

One cost-effective solution is to broaden the scope of the microfinance sector. Through recent policy prescriptions, the government has broadened the target market of microfinance providers. These policies were prompted by the realisation that given the low levels of formal borrowing in the country, a lot of potential customers were unbanked.

The Micro Units Development and Refinance Agency (MUDRA) Bank, a public sector financial institution, was set up in 2015 to enable commercial banks, regional rural banks, cooperative banks, NBFCs, and microfinance institutions under three categories to cater to microenterprises at different stages of their development, including the missing middle.

And on the legislative side, a bill was introduced in 2015 to amend the definitions of micro-, small-, and medium-sized enterprises. The bill proposes to increase the limits that determine the size of the enterprise. Given that the previous definition was set in 2006, this makes sense.

Bangladesh

Similar to India, the problem of financial exclusion is fairly prevalent in Bangladesh too. According to the World Bank's Global Findex database, only 35% of individuals above the age of 25 have an account and only 13% borrow from a formal financial institution.

However, Bangladesh is a pioneer in the field of microfinance and is very much considered to be its birthplace. The microfinance sector grew considerably in the 1990s until there were signs of maturity by 2008. Moreover, even though there are a large number of microfinance providers in the country, the supply of microcredit is highly concentrated with the three largest providers: Grameen Bank, ASA, and BRAC.

Financing options for MFI graduates in Bangladesh

As the microfinance market saturated in 2007, Bangladeshi MFIs realised the need to provide larger loans to members who can service them. And once they started offering these larger loans, they understood that demand came not only from members of the microfinance sector but also from other small business owners too, eager to climb the entrepreneurial ladder.

All MFIs can offer bigger loans. However, only the large- and medium-sized borrowers are able to access this segment owing to the scarcity of funding in smaller MFIs. Irrespective of the funding organisation, on top of the loans customers also receive education and training in basic financial practices.

The missing middle in Bangladesh

Despite Bangladesh being the pioneer in microfinance, the missing middle represents a significant gap for graduates. Taking into consideration the number of microenterprises in the country, the demand for financing is thought to hover around the $1.8 billion mark while current market supply caters for just over 60% of this.

Unlike India and Pakistan, MFIs in Bangladesh are able to address the MFI graduates, and the repayment rates for microenterprise loans appear to be excellent – reaching a very high score of 97.0%–99.5%.

A major handicap in the microfinance sector, however, is the absence of a credit bureau. In many cases, borrowers have taken loans from several MFIs (i.e. multiple borrowing). This means that MFIs are unable to ascertain the debt levels of potential borrowers, with the result that they have become risk-averse to handing out loans.

Policy initiatives in Bangladesh

The fact that MFIs are permitted to provide larger loans serves as a huge encouragement to potential MFIs and over the years increasing numbers of MFIs are becoming active in this segment. The large players still dominate the market though.

One such example is the Palli Karma-Sahayak Foundation (PKSF), a government organisation established to fund microfinance institutions in the country. Besides the government, PKSF also receives funding from the World Bank and donors around the globe. Over the years, PKSF has funded over $433 million to various microfinance institutions in the country.

In addition to funding, PKSF also implemented two programmes under the umbrella of the Finance for Enterprise Development and Employment Creation initiative to train MFIs on microenterprise appraisal and lending, strengthen microenterprise value chains, and provide business management training for micro-entrepreneurs.

The situation in Pakistan

Among the countries under research, Pakistan suffers the most from financial exclusion. According to the World Bank's Global Findex database, only 13% of individuals above the age of 25 have an account and only 2% have a formal borrowing account. The numbers call for an immediate and significant course of action from stakeholders in the sector.

Microfinance in Pakistan comprises three main categories: MFIs, rural support programmes, and microfinance banks. For their part, MFIs are non-banks – NGOs typically incorporated as trusts, societies, or non-profit companies. These organisations are not allowed to take deposits and are primarily involved in microcredit activities. Rural support programmes (RSPs) are rural-based NGOs that provide microfinance as part of a multidimensional programme for rural development though, here too, they are not allowed to take deposits. And finally, microfinance banks (MFBs) are licensed and supervised by the State Bank of Pakistan (SBP). Unlike MFIs and RSPs, MFBs can accept deposits from the public.

An uneven playing field

Things are far from smooth. RSPs and MFIs, unlike MFBs in Pakistan, are not actively supervised by the authorities they register with. Moreover, MFBs have the disadvantage of incurring higher costs for compliance with regulatory requirements than do RSPs and MFIs. However, this constitutes the price to pay for the exclusive advantage of MFBs to raise deposits.

As a way to level the playing field, SBP has permitted MFBs to extend their services to microenterprise loans. This allows MFBs to address their higher cost structure and compete with other players on the field. However, due to the different skill sets required to expand to the microenterprise sector, MFBs exercise caution before leaping.

Financing model and the missing middle in Pakistan

In general, loans from the microfinance sector are secured by deposits, government securities, or even gold – although unsecured loans are also offered based on the borrower's cash flow.

As many customers do not keep proper records and accounts, one of the organisation's key responsibilities is that of educating current and potential customers on how, among other matters, to differentiate between personal expenses and business expenses. The officers working for these organisations are trained to carry out the entire process from A to Z: going out in the field and interacting with customers to finalise the loan and the post-loan support.

Due to a lack of organised data, an estimate of the financing gap or the missing middle in Pakistan is unavailable. However, there are an approximated 3.8 million micro-, small-, and medium-sized enterprises in Pakistan, of which 70% are small enterprises. Most of them are expected to be unbanked.

Policy initiatives in Pakistan

The State Bank of Pakistan, along with the Government of Pakistan, has acknowledged the importance of microfinance providers offering enterprise loans to promote employment growth. This has resulted in permission for MFBs to seek approval to extend the size of microenterprise loans.

One area, for example, that has been the centre of microfinance focus is that of education and schools. Multiple, low-cost private schools have duly been established with the help of MFI aid and loans, and this constitutes an important aspect of the microenterprise landscape in Pakistan due to the challenges faced by the country in increasing school enrolment and literacy.

To further bolster the effort and act as a financial pipeline to MFIs, the Pakistan Microfinance Investment Company was created in 2016. This works as a hedge fund, mobilising funds from investors and channelling them into MFIs. Regarded as an important attempt to reduce the interest rate on microfinance loans, it renders them more attractive and accessible.

Microfinance as a grassroots solution

All three countries – India, Bangladesh, and Pakistan – have sizable missing middle segments with considerable employment potential. Given that growth in employment is such a key goal for all three, catering to the missing middle is a critical factor in shaping – and deciding – the future of the countries.

In all three countries, governments need to support lenders with funding options, make reporting to credit bureaus compulsory, and fund financial literacy campaigns targeted at microenterprises. Moreover, measures need to be implemented to reduce the use of cash-based transactions and make the registration of enterprises easier – and universal.

Will microfinance improve financial inclusion in these countries and accelerate economic growth? Or will it crumble before the challenges it faces? A combination of government support and efficient management provides a possible recipe to lead India, Bangladesh, and Pakistan to a sweeter and very promising future.

Key takeaways

- An inclusive financial system implies the availability of financial services for all income groups offering a range of financial services with no gaps in provision.
- There is a gap in the financial system of Bangladesh, India, and Pakistan that does not address the needs of MFI borrowers who outgrow microfinance and require larger loans that are not as large as Small and Medium Enterprises (SMEs).
- In India, in 2014, 56.3% of individuals above the age of 25 had an account and only 8.8% had a formal borrowing account.
- Financial exclusion is prevalent in Bangladesh, only 35% of individuals above the age of 25 having an account and only 13% borrowing from a formal financial institution.
- The fact that MFIs are permitted to provide larger loans in Bangladesh serves as a huge encouragement to the potential MFIs and over the years more MFIs are becoming active in this segment, though the large players dominate the market.
- Among the countries under consideration, Pakistan suffers the most from financial exclusion. Only 13% of individuals above the age of 25 have an account and only 2% have a formal borrowing account.
- In all three countries, governments need to support lenders with funding options, make reporting to credit bureaus compulsory, and fund financial literacy campaigns targeted at microenterprises.
- Measures need to be implemented to reduce the use of cash-based transactions and make the registration of enterprises easier – and universal.

Food for thought

- Why should traditional banks in emerging countries not fully cater for micro-enterprises? To what extent is this justified? How would you change this into a win–win?
- Imagine that you are in the government of one of the countries under study. What sort of incentives would you offer micro-enterprises to innovate, grow, create jobs, and provide tax revenue?

• To what extent can the small fish – micro-enterprises – benefit from and live in the company of larger or multinational companies? Is there room for a virtuous circle of cooperation? How?

Related research: *'Bridging the "Missing Middle" Between Microfinance and Small and Medium-Sized Enterprise Finance in South Asia', Asian Development Bank Institute Working Paper No. 587, July 2016.*

Micro case study 4: Finance

You are an advisor in a very traditional and reputed private bank. You receive the visit of one of your best clients, Mr. Dupont-Dupont, a retired ambassador. You have been advising him for some years. He is a prudent investor, and while initially reluctant to green investments, he gradually became more interested in the issue. Nowadays, in each of his visits, he likes to ask questions about green and socially responsible investments. The following is an excerpt from the discussion:

Mr. Dupont-Dupont: You know, I'm now quite fond of green investments, and I've been investing a part of my savings in those products. But, are you sure they pay off? I mean, compared to a conventional investment.

You: I would love to say a clear 'yes'. But the answer is more nuanced than that. There have been many studies, with different methodologies, and the results are not conclusive. To cut a long story short, the results of any investment vehicle, let's say a share, depends on many factors. I mean, macro-economic issues, competition among companies, the many decisions a company makes, and so on. Being more or less green may of course have an influence on results, but how much that influence is, that remains difficult to measure.

Mr. Dupont-Dupont: But at least I am not worse off.

You: Well, that's the nice part. To this day, and after many comparative studies, it doesn't seem that socially responsible investing has 'a cost', compared to conventional investments. Indeed, we may see that this kind of investment has become mainstream nowadays.

Mr. Dupont-Dupont: Well, I may imagine that a company that scores well in ESG issues has fewer risks. And that having a good ESG score can be a proxy for good management. I imagine that achieving good ESG scores is not easy, with only very well-managed companies able to do that.

You: And a well-managed company is precisely what you look for when you pick shares.

What do you think? Are there arguments for green/socially responsible investing being profitable, convenient, or less risky?

3 The role of the accountant, accounting, and new advances in reporting to reach the UN SDGs

Combating crises

How social and environmental accounting can build a future-proof economy

Charles H. Cho
Schulich School of Business, York University

Intertwined

Take a good look around, and you will see numerous examples of how we have transformed our world's landscape. We have cleared away millions of acres of forests, paved vast roads, built super-tall skyscrapers, created large plantations, and set up massive factories. In fact, nowadays, human beings have replaced nature as the dominant force shaping Earth. And is the widespread human impact on the planet a modern occurrence? The answer is no. We have been doing this since the beginning of civilisation.

Increasing levels of industrialisation, population, and urbanisation have resulted in a sharp increase in environmental concerns including climate change, air pollution, water depletion, and biodiversity destruction. Humanity is already existing outside the safe operating space for at least three of the nine planetary boundaries – namely the rate of biodiversity loss, climate change, and the nitrogen cycle.

Besides planetary degradation, researchers have also examined the impact of habitat destruction on global pandemics. According to the Chinese Center for Disease Control and Prevention, the new coronavirus (COVID-19) first appeared in Wuhan, China in December 2019 and it possibly came from wild animals. Sadly, virus transmissions from wild animal species to human beings happen frequently. But what are the circumstances that allow these diseases to jump from animals to humans?

Animal-to-human transmissions are not due to chance. It is a classic case of the old phrase, *what goes around comes around*. There is a growing consensus that ecological changes – including the human destruction of natural habitats and ecosystems – have led to increased rates of transmissions between animals and humans.

Due to the decrease in wildlife habitats, animal species are now forced to migrate into human-disturbed areas – suburbs, farmlands, and orchards, for instance – and be in closer contact with humans in order to survive, resulting

DOI: 10.4324/9781003317333-14

in a higher potential for contagion. These transmissions and the high COVID-19 mortality rate are most likely influenced by higher air pollution levels.

Unfortunately, the advent of the global COVID-19 pandemic in 2020 has magnified the effects of ongoing environmental destruction and made them even more obvious. Without a doubt, the COVID-19 pandemic is the biggest crisis since the Second World War, resulting in massive irretrievable human suffering all over the globe.

Smoke and mirrors

As an increasing number of countries entered lockdown, many personal and industrial activities were halted. Factories, shops, and schools were temporarily shut down. As a result of reduced activities, several positive impacts of the lockdown were reported, especially on the condition of beaches, the level of environmental noise, global CO_2 emissions, and air pollution.

As we know, nationwide lockdowns led to a temporary, and welcome, reduction in CO_2 emissions. International travel dropped to its lowest level in 75 years with more than 96% of flights being cancelled. It is calculated that more than half of the diminution in daily global CO_2 emissions in April 2020 is related to changes in surface transport. In addition, global air quality changes have also been linked to the imposed global traffic restrictions.

However, despite the broad range of short-term environmental improvements which became apparent during the pandemic, not all lockdown policies were as beneficial for the environment as they *appear* at first glance. In fact, several effects of COVID-19 have been more detrimental to the global environment in the long term.

However, the United Nations World Meteorological Organisation (WMO) recalled that this temporary cut in emissions is very small compared to the ongoing growing trend in greenhouse gases emissions. The WMO also reminded us that climate-heating gases are in any case reaching record levels.

A garbage crisis, too

Another significant environmental concern is the treatment of medical waste. As more disposable personal protective equipment (PPE) and other medical supplies were used all over the world, there are estimations of hospitals producing as much as six times more medical waste compared to normal, pre-pandemic times. It is an issue not only of how much waste but also of the nature of that waste. For instance, much of the needed material – medical supplies such as masks, gloves, and test kits – are made out of plastic. The very materials protecting us from infection could eventually cause harm to public health and the planet, as a large part of that material is single-use, and they end up in the ocean or in landfills.

Something fresh? Not quite

Governments all over the world have deployed new policy tools to deal with the COVID-19 crisis. Among them are economic stimulus packages, which in many cases include environmental considerations.

An example is the €750 billion recovery package – called Next Generation EU – adopted by the European Commission. Christened the 'biggest green stimulus in history', the initiative is directed to several areas, including expenditures earmarked to promoting energy efficiency and developing renewable energy resources, sustainable transport, and agriculture, among other measures of environmental protection.

Using economic stimulus packages is nothing new under the sun. For instance, in response to the 2008 financial crisis, around $3.3 trillion was allocated worldwide with 16% devoted to green measures – low carbon energy, pollution abatement, and materials recycling. In the EU, the European Economic Recovery Plan proposed by the European Commission in 2008, encouraged member countries to promote energy efficiency and investments in climate-friendly technologies with a total budget of around €200 billion.

Learning from failure

Despite those efforts, there was no long-term drop in carbon emissions. While they declined in 2009, they caught up the following year and eventually increased even more as the global economy returned to growth. Consequently, the economic stimulus package that the EU launched after the financial crisis did not achieve its environmental goals.

This crisis is different, but we can learn from the experience. We need to better assess the impacts of those stimulus packages on environmental results in the long run. For that, more ambitious transformations are needed.

The crux of the matter

The question arises: why are the most common responses to environmental crises unable to achieve the environmental transformation urgently needed on a global scale?

There are two reasons. First, there was no effective environmental monitoring of the previous EU stimulus programme. Second, sustainability goals tend to be subordinated to economic goals. Indeed, that package addressed specific industries and economic sectors, in a narrow approach. As a result, the deployed stimulus programmes often relied on accounting and accountability mechanisms that are ill-suited to achieve long-term environmental change.

The road to change

What insights can we draw from the example of the bygone failed EU stimulus programme and the current EU Green Deal in relation to its underlying accounting system? What would need to change within social and environmental accounting in order to address pressing environmental challenges?

- To begin with, capture ideas from a range of stakeholders when addressing sustainability. Any single account will not reflect the diversity of views and perspectives involved. Counter-accounts produced by external parties – expert reports, online journals, and NGOs, for instance – facilitate and encourage the voices of diverse interests. Those counter-accounts could give a clear message to companies, spurring much-needed improvements.
- Second, adopt a systems approach that takes into account the links and interactions between corporations, society, and ecology rather than treating organisations as individual entities detached from their natural environment.
- Third, use science-based targets and scenario planning to inform goal setting. Focus on indicators based on climate-related risks and dependencies.
- Next, a complete paradigm shift in understanding accountability as well as the functions and boundaries of traditional accounting techniques and tools is essential.
- Also, focus on how accountability can enlighten industries about the long-term risks and opportunities of a changing climate.
- Adopt a multidisciplinary and transdisciplinary approach to social and environmental accounting which brings on board the expertise of scientists, biologists, and scholars.
- Finally, push for substantial changes in education, courses, programmes, and curricula to allow outside-the-box thinking. The shift of mindset is more likely to happen at the training and education stage, transforming the way we teach future accountants, auditors, and managers, by blending into courses in ethical accounting, sustainable development, and stakeholder theory into traditional curricula. Also include participatory methods and multidisciplinary thinking – experiments, business modelling, and systems mapping – in programmes.

One small step for accounting, a giant step for humankind and the planet

The reality of current reports seems to indicate that the pandemic has made reaching 'net zero carbon' by 2050 even tougher to achieve. As economies roar back from the crisis and activity ramps up, billowing plumes of greenhouse gases will rise high into the sky, pollution levels will soar, the planet's resources will deplete further, and environmental destruction will grow. And the negative impact on society and humankind – Nature's revenge – will naturally follow. Who knows? Maybe we will find ourselves gazing long into the abyss of another disease soon enough.

Faced with this emergency, it is time to shed our denial and say goodbye to the business-and-habits-as-usual approach. The relevance of accounting and accountability cannot be overemphasised. With tremendous potential to offer transparent, inclusive, and ethically sound data at the intersection of business, government, society, and planet, accounting holds the golden key for the decision-makers of this world to make sound choices that are good for both humankind and nature.

Key takeaways

- Increasing levels of industrialisation, population, and urbanisation of our civilisations over time have resulted in a steep rise in environmental issues that include climate change, air pollution, water depletion, and destruction of our biodiversity.
- Humanity has transgressed at least three of the nine planetary boundaries necessary to establish a safe environmental operating space.
- At least 60% of emerging infectious diseases between 1960 and 2004 originate in non-human animals. There is increasing evidence that these animal-to-human transmissions are caused due to ecological changes triggered by human actions.
- In April 2020, during the early stages of the COVID-19 pandemic, daily CO_2 emissions had decreased by 17% compared to 2019 levels. But as countries emerge in 2021, pollution rates have never been as high.
- A significant environmental concern is the treatment of medical waste with hospitals producing six times more medical waste during 2020–early 2021 compared to pre-pandemic days. It is not only the quantity but also the type of waste that raises an alarm.
- Governments have tried to deal with crisis recovery through stimulus packages. However, these responses are limiting to achieve long-term sustainability change.
- New understandings of social and environmental value consistent with ecological principles are needed.
- Current accounting boundaries fail to reflect the interconnectivity of ecosystems.
- To lead to better outcomes of practice responses such as stimulus packages, adopt a systems approach rather than being restricted by a single

organisational focus; use science-based targets to inform goal setting; rethink adopted accountability mechanisms; and incorporate better education practices for future decision-makers and accountants.

Food for thought

- What do you think is the role of accounting in the transition towards a sustainable society?
- What are the shortcomings of your company's/organisation's current accounting approach?
- Which types of issues should you be looking at in order to create the sense of urgency that would prioritise the environment over conventional accounting consideration on a corporate level?

The everlasting image of the accountant as a constraining beancounter in popular culture

Mark Christensen and Sébastien Rocher
ESSEC Business School
IAE Nancy School of Management

Mr. Boulier, the iconic counterproductive beancounter

In the 1960s, in the comic book series *Gaston*, Belgian artist André Franquin narrates the fictional life of the comic book editing company Dupuis. Among the employees is Mr. Boulier, the accountant of the company. He is the archetype of a beancounter (as his name – Mr. Abacus in English – indicates it): a boring, conservative person. For example, after a cartoonist of the company asked for a new pencil to continue work on his drawing, Mr. Boulier, having issued a pencil earlier in the month, sternly refused the request. He then proceeded to unhelpfully advise the cartoonist to press less hard on his wooden pencil.

The creation of an accountant obsessed by costs and by the strict respect of rules whose counterproductive behaviour restricted creative work for a comics magazine was a way for Franquin to denounce and satirise the subordination of the artist to economic priorities.

The harmful beancounter over time

This stereotype was thus used to formulate an 'artist critique' of the profitability logic then reining in comics publishing firms. However, such a critique formulated via the image of a constraining beancounter was neither constant nor present across comic book history.

When artistic freedom was largest, that is to say when alternative comic books open the way for new kinds of artistic expression, like in the 1970s and at the end of the 1990s, this stereotype disappeared. During these periods, the accountant's behaviour became only a source of humour and when he was depicted as a beancounter, he was presented as someone with little power in the organisation.

This change can be explained by the recognition of cartoonists as artists and comics as art increased. As a consequence, it weakened the need

DOI: 10.4324/9781003317333-15

for portraits of accountants to complain about the dominant financial logic. As a result, the counterproductive dimension attached to the beancounter disappeared.

During the 1980s, however, circumstances began to change. Pressed by shareholder return demands, publishers skipped risky investments, thus cutting opportunities for cartoonists to develop innovative approaches. As a consequence, the harmful, counterproductive beancounter made a comeback.

L'Atelier Mastodonte or the everlasting image of the harmful beancounter

Since the 1990s, an alternative comics industry emerged. Its primary objective was to see comic books fully considered as artistic expressions rather than the product of the economic system, combined with a change of accountants' images in society, it can be expected that the image of the accounting seen as a constraining beancounter disappeared in popular culture.

This would be good news for the accounting profession whose legitimacy and attractiveness are hurt when accountants are depicted as constraining and counterproductive beancounters. Such an image is the opposite of the role they have nowadays in society and opposed to the image they want to convey to students as well as to their clients.

However, it is still possible to find the constraining beancounter stereotype in recent comic books. For example, *L'atelier Mastodonte* is a comic book that also tells the fictional life of a group of cartoonists within the Dupuis publishing house, in which appears the character of Mr. Caillez. So what are the grounds for the continued portrayal of this beancounter image?

L'Atelier Mastodonte is produced by a group of cartoonists. They tell the life of a fictitious studio they share within the Dupuis publishing company, via short humorous stories on half a page. The cartoonists are therefore simultaneously authors and protagonists of the story told. Concretely, a cartoonist publishes a short comic, then one or several others react by imagining a sequel from their point of view, which will call for other reactions, and so on.

The analysis of this collective work thus makes it possible to collect the point of view of a group of cartoonists by looking at the possible variations that they give to the character of Mr. Caillez, who was taken up by seven different cartoonists. Moreover, the artist caricaturing himself as a member of the studio allows to grasp how is conceived the relationship of the cartoonist to the accountant.

The analysis carried out within the framework of this study was based on the comics of the three cartoonists who most referred to the character of Mr. Caillez, namely Lewis Trondheim (8 stories), Pascal Jousselin (8 stories), and Jerôme Jouvray (3 stories, including 1 in 3 pages and not on half a page), that is to say, 20 of the 26 stories in which Mr. Caillez appears.

In order to analyse the reasons for the profile given to this character, Iconology, a popular method of studying the content and meanings of visuals, has been used to peel off the layers of the artwork.

Mr. Caillez, the archetypal counterproductive beancounter

M. Caillez is a rigid man, never smiling except when reducing costs. For instance, when there was the opportunity to replace the existing comics with poor imitations costing less money. As such, he was the defender of commercial logic, only looking for profits at the expense of artistic values.

Above all, he does not realise that he is counterproductive. For example, he advises an author to sell his originals in order to increase his income, like this well-known cartoonist whose name he has lost who draws the adventures of a reporter with his little dog. The cartoonist replies that Hergé (one of the most famous cartoonists in the history of comics) is dead, but Mr. Caillez only sees a lack of effort on the part of the cartoonist. In the same way, in order to save money, under the cover of ecological logic, he suggests that the bleached paper be replaced by recycled paper (even though ink smears on recycled paper), that the heating be limited (even if the artists must draw with mittens on their hands), as well as the use of computer tools (even if the computer has replaced the sheet and the pen for some authors), in order to save electricity.

The Caillez character reflected a willingness to challenge a predominant financial logic in the comics industry. This allowed the cartoonist to display his personal status and authenticity as an artist while still working with a conventional publisher.

The message behind the laughable character

If the behavioural characteristics of this character are shared by all the cartoonists, the use of this character with regard to the message conveyed differs.

Lewis Trondheim always represents himself as the interlocutor of Mr. Caillez in a respectful relationship between the two characters. This relationship, devoid of any dimension of power of one over the other, can be explained by the status of Lewis Trondheim in the microcosm of the

French-speaking comics world: he is an artist benefiting from a great notoriety, as much among comics fans as among other cartoonists, a situation of which he is aware (he represents himself, for example, passing in front of an art gallery whose owner asks him for drawings, a sign of artistic recognition). He is therefore not in a situation of dependence on the publishing company (represented by Mr. Caillez), but in a partnership relationship.

With the alternative comics' successes, publishing companies allowed more open editorial policies, with larger room for artistic initiative. At the same time, they also sought to attract cartoonists from the alternative movement. Lewis Trondheim is one of the cartoonists who migrated from the small press/alternative comics industry to the historically established publishers.

Mr. Caillez is more than a character to make readers laugh at the limits of a financial logic pushed to excess. The Caillez character allows the artist to display his status as an artist by showing that they are not sold to the economic logic of the large editing company. This shows that it is possible to maintain one's status as an artist while working in the domain of large-scale cultural production.

Pascal Jousselin represents Mr. Caillez as a constraint for the artist because he does not understand the art world nor the difficulties of artists. In his stories in which Mr. Caillez appears, he denounces the working conditions of cartoonists. For example, he tries to explain to Mr. Caillez the working conditions of cartoonists and concludes: 'financially, it's better to clean a comic book publishing company's toilets than to make comic books'. Mr. Caillez replied that he understood and that he would find a solution. And Pascal Jousselin appears, in the last panel of the story, busy cleaning the toilets of the publishing company.

Mr. Caillez also overhears a discussion between Pascal Jousselin and another member of the company, in which the two of them agree on the exploitation of cartoonists by editing companies and want to find concrete ways to fight this situation. Mr. Caillez starts to sweat. But as the artists sit down to think, they find a comic book in progress on the table. They forget their desire to rebel and discuss how to improve this comic book. Mr. Caillez can leave reassured.

Thus, although Pascal Jousselin uses this beancounter character to denounce the working condition of cartoonists, this character also allows him to show that what matters to him above all is his taste for comics and that he does not do this job for the money. He thus uses the accountant to show that he defends a logic of 'art for art's sake', far from a commercial logic.

In a parody of Superman in which Jérôme Jouvray plays the American superhero, he confronts the villain, Mr. Caillez, over a question of an outstanding bill. The cartoonist justifies his delay by the fact that he has illustrations to finish. The opposition of the logic of the accountant as an enemy of the artist transpires from this sequence. At the end of the story, back in the studio, Mr. Caillez brings a bill to Jérôme Jouvray and unfortunately spills his inkwell on his work. It is possible to read the constraint of the artist and his subjection to the financial logic (the accountant and the quest for money destroys art). Moreover, this intervention of the accountant during the realisation of a comic book can be understood as an absence of freedom, an omnipresent constraint in the artistic work.

In another story, the editor-in-chief reads a note from Mr. Caillez to the cartoonist. Mr. Caillez is trying to save money under the guise of an ecological logic, even if it means being counterproductive; Jérôme Jouvray asks Lewis Trondheim to take the side of cartoonists. But Lewis Trondheim, rather than being in opposition, adapts to these new conditions. If the editor-in-chief editor is delighted with such a behaviour, the cartoonists see Lewis Trondheim as being sold to the economic interests of the publishers.

Artist and social critiques and the quest for artistic authenticity

Lewis Trondheim, Pascal Jousselin, and Jérôme Jouvray use the character of the beancounter to put forward their authenticity and their artistic approach which responds to the logic of 'art for art's sake'. They perceive the beancounter as the incarnation of the capitalist logic of which they provide an artistic criticism coupled with a social criticism by taking up the following four sources of indignation:

(a) capitalism as a loss of authenticity
(b) capitalism as a loss of freedom
(c) capitalism as a source of misery
(d) capitalism as a source of opportunism, selfishness, and the destruction of social ties and solidarity.

While these three cartoonists take up the same criticisms that Franquin was already formulating through Mr. Boulier, their aim is however different: it is no longer a question of denouncing a bad situation but of defining oneself as an artist based on a simulacrum of criticism since Mr. Caillez is not the evocation of the accountant of the comics publishing company Dupuis, whereas it was the case for Mr. Boulier.

With great power comes great responsibility

Comics are a central feature of mass culture. They are easy to read and widely accessible. A persistent art form that reflects society, comics highlight important economic, social, political, and cultural problems of the time to arouse the satirical consciousness of its readers.

The idea of the rigid beancounter has been used as social critique, going well beyond the role of accountants and accounting, including among others, concerns about the role of artists, and the tensions between profits and creativity.

On the one hand, viewing accounting from the perspective of popular culture strengthens the idea that the beancounter image would not go on forever. On the other hand, it also cannot be slated that the ghost of the accountant stereotyped as a constraining beancounter be laid to rest. Boulier may be here to stay awhile!

Key takeaways

- Artists crafted the image of the accountant to serve different functions over time and to make comments on issues much wider than accountancy.
- The image of the accountant as a rigid beancounter implied a criticism of publishing firms based primarily on profits logic.
- In recent years, during the acceptance of the alternative comics, the beancounter came back as a way for artists to claim authenticity while opposing the profitability focus of publishing firms.
- In spite of efforts to change the perception of the accounting profession, the beancounter image remains a recurrent challenge.

Food for thought

- What is your perception/experiences with the accountant professionals in your company/organisation? Do they fit a stereotype?
- How can accounting firms entice the young into a profession that has a reputation for the dull and dreary?
- How can educational institutes possibly attempt to portray the Accounting subject in a thrilling manner?

Triple capital accounting
Putting a price on the planet and people

Raphaël Hara and Adrien Covo
Ksapa

In dire straits

The world has entered the Anthropocene, the 'age of humans', where the economy exerts phenomenal pressure on Earth. Human beings have become the single most influential species on the planet, causing significant changes to land, environment, water, organisms, and the atmosphere. Indeed, the latest 2022 Intergovernmental Panel on Climate Change (IPCC) report points towards our responsibility in this and the fact that we are already suffering from the effects of climate change.

We are all well aware of the gloomy list of perils of the 21st century, with awareness of the intimate and interwoven links between business, climate, nature, digital, human rights, and even the COVID crisis.

In 2009, an international team of researchers at the Stockholm Resilience Centre identified several processes that regulate the stability of the Earth system. These include the atmospheric concentration of greenhouse gases, the oceanic power of hydrogen, and the integrity of the biosphere. Through the pressures human activities exert on these processes, the resilience of the Earth system is now at risk. This ultimately threatens our planet's capacity to sustain desirable living conditions for the human species, which could lead to deterioration of human well-being in many parts of the world.

And that's not all. We simultaneously face huge social challenges. Consider the recurrence of economic and financial crises and ever-increasing wealth inequalities. So many considerations have come to challenge the sustainability of our economic and financial models.

As a result, the last few decades have witnessed the emergence of tools intended to reposition the role of companies in society. Others seek to rebalance activities through a better consideration of their socio-economic and environmental impacts, both positive and negative. For instance, that is how environmental taxes came into being. However, most measures

DOI: 10.4324/9781003317333-16

remain driven by economic considerations, from taxes to markets and labour costs, etc.

A long way to go

Although non-financial reporting is rapidly evolving, a lot remains to be done in the area of accounting standards.

Accounting is of prime importance to economic players as it guides corporate and investment policies. For the same reason, accounting methods are grounded in a highly capitalistic vision of the company. Firms mainly account on the basis of the financial bottom line, which means that more often than not, environmental and social externalities are neglected. This presents business with a dilemma . . . namely, balancing making a profit – after all, that's what the core of business is about – and preserving the planet from which it derives the very resources it depends on to operate.

With the rebalancing of priorities considering our current climate and social emergency, it has become fairly mainstream for private resources to be directed with the 2030 UN Sustainable Development Goals in mind. Given this compass bearing – among others – the accounting field is putting its money where its mouth is to play a role in financing the global agenda. That is exactly the goal of triple capital accounting (TCA).

Counting what really counts

TCA is designed to reflect the impacts of corporate activities, not just in terms of financial capital but also on natural and human assets – for instance, the environmental and psychological impacts of work and accidents. At its core, triple capital accounting is based on a strong sustainability principle across all environmental and societal matters. If a company's activities damage the environment, then it must account for the maintenance expenditure required by the corresponding environmental restoration efforts.

One of TCA's key principles is to apply the powerful strategy of capital preservation to human and social capital. For example, we are used to the concepts of depreciation as well as reinvestment and capital expenditure, in order to maintain and develop the key assets of a company that are displayed on the balance sheet. Traditional accounting requires the financial capital to be preserved before establishing that the business has made a profit and paying out dividends. TCA applies the same logic to natural and social capital – strategic assets that companies should not forget about.

Including natural and human capital in liabilities guarantees the conservation of such assets with the same scrutiny as with financial capital. Since it is essential to maintain the integrity of this capital as well, all capital is considered independent and non-substitutable.

As such, TCA expands a company's understanding of its own assets. It effectively allows firms to present themselves in a new light and highlight an aspect of their business model investors or stakeholders previously undervalued.

The sum and substance

A direct application of TCA is the CARE-TDL method (Comprehensive Accounting in Respect of Ecology – Triple Depreciation Line), created by Prof. Jacques Richard. CARE addresses profit generation without incurring damages to corporate human, environmental, and financial capital.

The model operates around the following six principles/axioms:

1. Social Axiom 1 (SA1) = The economy is dependent on three capitals – financial, natural, and human – to function and they deserve to be preserved.
2. SA2 = To maintain a capital, it is necessary to describe and apprehend it in the best way possible. For instance, what does it mean to preserve it, what is the impact that we can have on this capital, and what do we do in relation to this impact? Key indicators must be identified for each asset and appropriate conservation thresholds should be defined.
3. Accounting Axiom 1 (AA1) = For the sake of preservation, all three capital assets are recorded as liabilities on the balance sheet. Their use implies an obligation for the company to safeguard them as well.
4. AA2 = Their use necessarily implies deterioration. All three capital sources are included as resources but are systematically depreciated.
5. AA3 = Asset use and preservation must be reflected in financial statements, particularly balance sheets and income statements.
6. AA4 = CARE's guiding principle is that the measurement of any capital is determined by the cost of its preservation.

Every 'step' of the way

The purpose of the CARE model is not to attribute value to nature or to damages caused but to finance the preservation of both ecosystems and people. There are four steps to the framework.

1. Define natural and human capital

   • Identify sources of natural and human capital and their respective indicators
   • Define relevant preservation thresholds

2. Measure the preservation level of capital

    • Collect organisational socio-environmental data
    • Compare collected data against preservation thresholds

3. Optimise for the socio-ecological transition

    • Develop scenarios to observe these thresholds
    • Decide on the basis of a cost–benefit analysis

4. Value overall performance

    • Embed natural and human capital in corporate accounting
    • Disclose overall performance.

Prime movers

External stakeholders must be extensively involved in order to aptly define assets under consideration, indicators as well as scenarios. Stakeholder dialogue also enables teams to design and verify their approach, and develop a triple-capital balance sheet. Among others, target stakeholders include employees, non-profits, water and soil treatment agencies, and scientists.

Before any effective accounting can take place, a company must acquire a sound understanding of the socio-environmental issues linked to its activities. This depends on nurturing a strong ecosystem of stakeholders. Bearing in mind the lengthy processes of accounting and change management associated with the CARE method, such a transition can only happen in phases. It should start as a pilot project, which can later be extended to the entire organisation once the implementation methodology is sufficiently refined.

Achilles heel

The CARE model has its limitations. Because it depends on preservation costs to account for natural and human capital, the method fails to encompass the positive externalities of the regenerative economy – one that fully rebuilds any resources it uses, and repairs previously done damage to the ecosystem. In effect, if the land upon which an investor sets up operation is degraded from the get-go, focusing on maintenance costs no longer makes sense. That investor would in fact have to finance land regeneration to exploit it. While this would eventually result in positive externalities, it cannot currently be translated into the CARE framework.

Wait, there's more

Several other methodologies that investigate people and environmental dimensions on top of conventional profit can be highlighted.

Universal Accounting (Saint-Front): The model measures the value created for players in any given territory, making stakeholder engagement an integral component of its development. This entails stakeholders be clearly identified and their priorities listed. A process of co-creation is initiated to design relevant indicators for each key issue as well as the corresponding measurement processes. The data is then translated into monetary figures and aggregated into income statements for each stakeholder. An overall profit and loss statement ultimately includes all proposed indicators.

At its core, the Universal Accounting model is primarily intended to monetise the impact of corporate responsibility programmes. As such, selected indicators and strategies are divided into four accounting areas of governance, social rights, the environment, and society. None can mutually compensate another. So, a strong sustainability principle is followed.

Environmental Profit & Losses (Puma, Kering): The EP&L is an income statement designed to measure the environmental impact of supply chain activities. This environmental footprint takes into account water consumption, carbon emissions, water pollution, land use, air pollution, and waste production. The resulting data is then converted into monetary values to convey an overview of the costs of all corporate activities.

This method internalises negative externalities and monetises the cost borne by the environment for each activity. This is achieved by accounting for the ecosystem services on which a company depends to function, in addition to the cost of direct and indirect negative impacts on the environment. This supports a comprehensive understanding of the magnitude of these impacts and their location along the value chain.

Natural Capital Protocol (Natural Capital Coalition): The Natural Capital Protocol is a decision-making framework for businesses to identify, measure, and evaluate their impacts and interdependencies with nature. The tool helps companies measure and embed natural capital considerations in existing processes, including those pertaining to their risk management, supply chain management, or product design.

The cornerstone for resilient business

The importance of measuring the socio-environmental impact of economic activities cannot be overstated. If companies want to ensure their businesses sustain and perform as well as make the economy resilient to risks in the future, it is important that they put 'caring for Earth and people' on the top of their agenda, and redesign accounting models to fit a world with limits. So, are you among the ones to take the leap?

Key takeaways

- While non-financial reporting is rapidly evolving, accounting standards reforms still have a way to go before they fully account for socio-environmental issues.
- Accounting offers a prime comprehension tool for key economic players, its fundamentals, and core methods guiding corporate and investment policies.
- The UN Sustainable Development Goals act as a primary compass for companies who have to integrate human and natural assets in their accounting.
- Triple capital accounting (TCA) is designed to reflect the impact of corporate activities and is based on a strong sustainability principle across all environmental and societal matters.
- If a firm's activities damage the environment, then it must account for the maintenance expenditure entailed by the corresponding environmental restoration efforts.
- The CARE-TDL framework, a direct application of TCA, addresses profit generation without incurring damages to corporate human, environmental, and financial capital.
- External stakeholders must be involved in the governance processes in order to properly define assets under consideration, indicators as well as scenarios.
- Stakeholder dialogue allows teams to design and verify their approach to develop a triple-capital balance sheet.
- Other accounting methodologies include Universal Accounting (Saint-Front); Environmental Profit & Losses (Puma, Kering); and Natural Capital Protocol (Natural Capital Coalition).

Food for thought

- Given the insights into the various sustainable accounting methodologies, which one do you think would most suit your company/organisation and why?
- To what end would such a financial statement be of use to your organisation? How would it help your organisation in terms of strategy and development?
- To what extent should such accounting become mandatory in addition to traditional accounting obligations?

Value-added statements

A powerful reporting tool for corporate sustainability

Adrián Zicari
ESSEC Business School

A recent 'big deal'

Until recently, most large businesses were driven almost exclusively with a single goal in mind: profit. Maximising profits for shareholders and executives was at the heart of every action taken or initiative pursued.

In the past few decades, however, more firms have recognised that they also have a social responsibility – to do what's best not just for their companies, but for people, the planet, and society at large.

Firms have an interest in showing what their positive impact is on all stakeholders. It could be that companies act proactively out of an ethical duty. They might also think that they can contribute to improving the world through their products and activities. And they certainly believe that positive communication is good for their organisation and that, in the end run, investors will prefer to commit money to a company that is socially aligned.

A tangled web

Corporate social responsibility (CSR) – as with many concepts – has variants, if not different schools of thought, according, not least, to where you live in the world. It is a complex notion, one that is hard to measure.

Its inherent complexity has led to the outlook that traditional financial accounting is incapable of presenting a clear picture of CSR performance. This has resulted in a wave of 'new' reporting models or 'extended financial reporting' such as the Global Reporting Initiative (GRI) to capture dimensions of corporate performance that are not well addressed by traditional financial indicators.

There's more than meets the eye

However, this view is challenged: while stakeholders may well benefit from these new models, conventional accounting can still offer them valuable

DOI: 10.4324/9781003317333-17

insights concerning CSR performance. That means traditional and new accounting perspectives are complementary instead of being opposed.

Let's put the spotlight on the ongoing experience of several Latin American firms with value-added statements (VAS) – a kind of social report based on conventional accounting. It was Luis Perera Aldama who, in his role at PricewaterhouseCoopers, tailored a particular model of VAS which he christened 'The Fourth Financial Statement'. The tool is now used by over 15 firms in Latin America to show how companies create and distribute value among stakeholders.

Interestingly, this innovation is particularly suited to the continent and its emerging economies. Further, it is a tool that can quite relevantly be used by emerging countries on other continents. This is because the concerns of emerging countries are weighted differently from those of already advanced economies: economic development is needed in order to close the gap with industrialised countries, while at the same time income distribution needs to improve.

A walk down history lane

Value-added reports are not at all new. The Fourth Financial Statement model finds its precursor in the UK in the late 1970s and early 1980s. The sudden increase of interest in VAS reporting was sparked by the discussion paper presented by the Institute of Chartered Accountants in England and Wales. The report revolutionised the landscape by identifying that not only shareholders but seven different groups of stakeholders had 'a reasonable right to information and whose information needs should be recognised by corporate reports' (ASSC, 1975).

In the years following the paper, a significant number of UK firms published VAS documents. But this phenomenon rapidly disappeared with the coming to power of the Thatcher government in 1979. A similar pattern was witnessed in Spain: a surge in interest that eventually waned. These events suggest that VAS reporting seems to emerge with underperforming or emerging economies rather than established and vibrant ones. Indeed, the financial crises of 2009 and 2011 once again saw a resurgence of VAS, this time in Latin America. One of the VAS models now used there is the Fourth Financial Statement.

Ins and outs

The Fourth Financial Statement builds on existing VAS models and promotes a simple idea: a breakdown of the profit and loss (P&L) statement into value creation and value distribution. First, sales revenue minus direct costs needed for product/service creation is considered in order to obtain an estimate of value creation. Second, the distribution of this value among stakeholders – employees, shareholders, taxes, banks and financial suppliers, and the community and environment – is displayed. The distribution pattern clearly shows the economic impact of the firm on society by making explicit the proportion of value received by each stakeholder.

The Fourth Financial Statement is unique, too, in that it is accompanied by a collection of additional notes related to sustainability/CSR issues. And beautifully simple in that data for the statement comes from conventional accounting.

It is interesting to note that the name adopted for this model is intentionally provocative. It suggests making the VAS document an integral part of the annual set of accounts of a firm. As such, this document accompanies and complements the three traditional financial statements – balance, P&L, and cash flow.

Shining examples in action

Among the increasing number of companies using the Fourth Financial Statement model is BHP Billiton, a British-Australian mining company, which has been using this model for some years for its division in Chile. The experience showed that producing the report the first time around calls for great effort due to the need to analyse vast amount of information and for the financial team to become familiarised with the model. The initiative was a success. Managers at the time felt that the Fourth Statement presents business results in a simple way and facilitates the communication of CSR-related performance to both internal and external stakeholders.

Another example, Sociedades Bolívar, a large holding company for insurance and mortgage loans in Colombia, has been using the model for many years in most of its business units. The firm's managers from both accounting and CSR areas worked together in the implementation of this model – a sharp contrast to the classic situation whereby sustainable reporting is a project 'toy' of CSR managers only. Additionally, the company management considers the Fourth Statement as a way of shaping dialogue with stakeholders: in this way, each party can have a more complete comprehension of what the company does, and which issues are particularly relevant for each one.

Kimberly Clark, the manufacturer of personal and healthcare products and a recognised leader with regard to CSR issues, has been using the Fourth Statement for its Andean division. They consider the Fourth Statement as a facilitator for stakeholder dialogue, making CSR an integral part of the business model and not just the concern of one particular department.

EPM, a large energy company in Colombia, sees the Fourth Statement not as an alternative but as a complement to other sustainability reporting tools. EPM has been using the Fourth Statement as an internal reporting device: it is both a key component of its corporate scorecard and a planning tool, as the company regularly prepares projections on this model. In a similar vein, ANTEL, the state-owned telephone company of Uruguay, has for long been using the Fourth Statement.

Towards a fifth dimension?

Research and assessment of the Fourth Financial Statement in action focus mainly on large firms, though the model can also be used in small- and medium-sized companies. It may also be of especially relevant use for emerging economies given the argument that CSR adapts to, and evolves differently in, different parts of the world. Moreover, as CSR has its origins in developed countries, it tends to be focused on its own roots while ignoring or de-emphasising priorities in emerging countries. As such, the future might well see VAS being used in Africa and various parts of Asia and adapted to local practices and specifics.

As it happens with any other organisational changes, implementing the Fourth Statement implies leadership from top managers, support from the whole organisation, and support from IT systems.

The beauty of the model lies in its applicability, not only as a CSR reporting tool but also as a means of defining how to manage the firm's business and pursue different distribution strategies. For instance, a firm may choose to pay higher average salaries, while another could choose to have more people on its payroll. Similarly, a company may choose to buy more from local vendors, invest more, or monitor the consequences of its pricing policy. These different actions, which represent different approaches to CSR, are more clearly illustrated by the Fourth Statement.

Despite the challenges of getting people to work with each other across departments, and despite the still common temptation to outsource social reporting to third parties, implementations of the Fourth Financial Statement tend to be successful.

It becomes the report of all those working in the firm – a far cry from the typical situation in which a sustainability report remains the isolated action of a highly professional CSR team, with scarce impact among stakeholders. It represents an innovative answer to the burning issue of inequality in Latin America, and a way of 'walking the talk' by showing meaningful information. All in all, VAS and the Fourth Financial Statement model add a new, innovative, practical, and motivating dimension to CSR in firms.

Key takeaways

- Traditional accounting, and more specifically the value-added statement (VAS), can be a useful tool that complements CSR measurement.
- The VAS or Fourth Financial Statement shows how companies create value and how that value is distributed among each category of stakeholder – employees, government, finance suppliers, community and environment, and shareholders.
- The Fourth Financial Statement implies that it should be used as an integral part of the firm's annual accounts, accompanying and complementing the traditional other three statements: balance, P&L, and cash flow.
- It breaks down the profit and loss (P&L) statement into how much value a company creates and how it distributes that value.
- To obtain an estimate of the value creation, sales revenue minus direct costs linked to creating the product or service is calculated.
- The distribution of this value is then displayed in the various sums paid to different company stakeholders.
- In this way, the distribution pattern clearly shows the economic impact of the firm on society by making explicit the proportion of value received by each stakeholder.
- The Fourth Financial Statement is cost-friendly for firms, although producing the statement the first time around calls for time and effort due to the need to analyse large amounts of information and for the financial team to become familiarised with the model.
- The beauty of the model lies in its applicability, not only as a CSR reporting tool but as a way of defining how to manage the firm's business and pursuing different distribution strategies.
- Because all the firm's financial dimensions are included, it is a model that all the firm's employees can relate to and identify with.

Food for thought

- Why should your company/organisation wish to draw up a Fourth Financial Statement? What would be the possible gains from doing this?
- The Fourth Financial Statement might be a way of encouraging employees to become interested in their firm's impact. To what extent do you agree with this statement? How? Why?
- How can you involve employees more in CSR-related activities and issues?

Further reading

Accounting Standards Steering Committee (1975) *The Corporate Report*, The Institute of Chartered Accountants in England and Wales, London

Aldama, Perera and Adrián Zicari (2012) Value-added reporting as a tool for sustainability: A Latin American experience. *Corporate Governance, the International Journal of Business in Society*, Vol. 12, Iss: 4, pp. 485–498

The EU green taxonomy

A common language for sustainability

Farid Baddache
Ksapa

Code red for humanity

Climate change is affecting the entire planet. People are witnessing first-hand the impacts of more extreme weather. The deadly heat waves, intense wildfires, gargantuan hurricanes, and other disasters that are happening on an increasingly regular basis are impossible to ignore. And while the world has been plunged into a deadly pandemic, scientists are sounding a deafening alarm that the worst is yet to come – thanks to humanity's 'stewardship' of the planet. The previous two UN IPCC (Intergovernmental Panel on Climate Change) endorse this – we are the culprits and we're already seeing the damage.

The European Union aims to be climate neutral by 2050. To help that process, it has come up with the European Green Deal, a set of policies to direct investments towards sustainable projects. The fundamental tool of the European Green Deal is the EU Green Taxonomy, which seeks to provide clarity for companies, investors, and policymakers on which economic activities are sustainable.

Yardsticks

This new Taxonomy sets performance thresholds, or 'technical screening criteria', for economic activities which:

1. Contribute substantially to at least one of six environmental goals. These range from climate change mitigation to climate change adaptation, sustainable protection of water and marine resources, the circular economy transition, pollution prevention and control, and the protection and restoration of biodiversity and ecosystems.
2. Do no significant harm (DNSH) to any of the other five goals wherever relevant.

DOI: 10.4324/9781003317333-18

3. Meet minimum safeguards (e.g. OECD Guidelines on Multinational Enterprises and the UN Guiding Principles on Business and Human Rights).

These performance thresholds help companies, project promoters, and issuers access green financing to improve their environmental performance. Additionally, it supports them in identifying environmentally friendly activities. In doing so, it helps to grow low-carbon sectors and decarbonise their high-carbon counterparts.

As such, the Green Taxonomy is supportive of the EU's 2030 climate and energy targets. It offers a new classification system designed to shift investments towards a low-carbon and climate-resilient economy – as opposed to greenwashing.

The bedrock

The Taxonomy Regulation (TR) creates a legal basis for the Green Taxonomy by setting out its overarching framework and environmental objectives. It also issues new legal obligations for financial market participants, large companies, the EU, and Member States.

Secondary legislation, called delegated acts, includes detailed technical screening criteria which supplement the TR. Following this criterion, private players can pinpoint which of their economic activities may be deemed sustainable.

On the radar

By defining screening criteria, the Green Taxonomy develops a list of environmentally sustainable activities. That said, it is a rating of neither 'good' or 'bad' companies. Nor is it a mandatory list of economic activities to invest in or to divest from. It does, however, aim to provide clear definitions of what constitutes 'green' for companies, investors, and policymakers.

The Taxonomy Regulation lays out three groups of Green Taxonomy users:

- Financial market participants, including occupational pension providers, that offer and distribute financial products in the EU
- Large companies already required to publish non-financial disclosures under the Non-Financial Reporting Directive (NFRD)
- The EU and Member States upon setting public measures, standards, or labels for green financial products or green (corporate) bonds.

New essentials

The final Taxonomy Regulation introduces a new disclosure requirement for users of the second category.

The NFRD covers, at minimum, large public-interest companies with more than 500 employees. This includes listed companies, banks, and insurance companies. Any company subject to this requirement will have to describe how and to what extent their activities are aligned to the Taxonomy.

For instance, non-financial corporate disclosures must now include:

- The proportion of turnover derived from the Taxonomy activities; and
- Their capital expenditure and, if relevant, operating expenditure associated with Taxonomy activities.

Such disclosures are to be embedded in non-financial statements, included in annual reports or separate sustainability reports.

Play by the rules

Companies and other issuers disclosing against the EU Green Taxonomy will be required to assess their compliance with minimum quantitative and process-based, qualitative criteria. The latter include standards embedded in the OECD Guidelines on Multinational Enterprises and the UN Guiding Principles on Business and Human Rights, with specific reference to the ILO Core Labor Conventions.

Private players will also be expected to check their compliance with the technical screening criteria for avoiding significant harm to environmental objectives. Core regulatory and standards of reference include EU regulations as well as the ISO 31000:2018 Risk Management and ISO 14015:2010 Environmental Management guidelines.

Far-reaching effects

Companies based in, doing business with, or working with investors in the EU are bound to heed the Green Taxonomy and anticipate major impacts on investments.

The TR is likely to increase investment in activities deemed environmentally sustainable across a range of sectors. This includes (but is not limited to) food and agriculture, construction and real estate, technologies, capital-intensive industries, transport, energy and utilities, consumer goods, and financial services. This covers virtually every business line with major impacts on the climate. In other words, the Green Taxonomy is a big deal for any company based in Europe, doing business or investing in the European market.

Travelling down the green brick road

Implementation of the Taxonomy requires that financial actors run a five-step check process. An example of how this applies to investments in companies is as follows:

1. Identify activities conducted by the company or issuer as well as those covered by financial products (e.g. projects and use of proceeds) that are potentially aligned with the Green Taxonomy. Also, consider which of its six environmental objective(s) they address.
2. Verify whether the company or issuer meets the relevant screening criteria for each activity. For example, is the electricity generation below 100 gCO2e/kWh?
3. Ensure all DNSH criteria are met by the issuer. Investors using the Green Taxonomy will most likely use a due diligence-type process to review the performance of underlying investees. They may rely on the legal disclosures of eligibility from those investees to that end.
4. Conduct due diligence to avoid any violation of the social minimum safeguards stipulated in the Taxonomy Regulation.
5. Calculate your investments' alignment with the Taxonomy and prepare disclosures at the investment product level.

It's time to change the game

Species extinction, disease, heatwaves, ecosystem collapse, rising seas, and other devastating climate impacts are accelerating and have become painfully obvious. There are increasing calls for substantial reduction of these adverse impacts – urging financial institutions and investors to focus on where they invest, fund, and finance to ensure they do not do significant harm across these activities.

As financial institutions embark on a new journey, they have to focus on new frameworks, guidelines, and methodologies which bring in more transparency to the world of finance. The EU Green Taxonomy is a good place to start.

The Taxonomy offers a common language and granular definition of what 'green' activities are. The corresponding screening criteria are useful tools to lend financial institutions and investors greater clarity and certainty on the environmental sustainability of different types of investments.

In essence, the EU Green Taxonomy is a clear game changer for both companies and investors alike. And one that should be embraced for the benefits it brings to business, planet, and society.

Key takeaways

- The EU taxonomy is a tool to help investors, companies, issuers, and project promoters navigate the transition to a low-carbon, resilient, and resource-efficient economy.
- The TR states three different groups of users for whom it will be mandatory to comply with the taxonomy regulation.

  - Financial market participants that offer financial products in the EU
  - Large companies that are already required to report non-financial information under the scope of the Non-Financial Reporting Directive (NFRD)
  - The EU and Member States when setting public measures, standards, or labels for green financial products or green bonds.

- Applying the Taxonomy to assess if investments are aligned with the EU's environmental objectives requires a careful step-by-step approach.

  1) Identify companies with activities that could be aligned to one or more environmental objectives.
  2) Check if the substantial contribution criteria are met.
  3) Check if the 'do no significant harm' criteria are met.
  4) Check if there are any negative impacts on minimum safeguards.
  5) Calculate the alignment of investment with the Taxonomy.

Food for thought

- How does the EU Taxonomy help your industry sector/company/organisation transition towards sustainability?
- To what extent do you have the necessary resources to implement the Taxonomy?
- How can your company/organisation benefit from having Taxonomy-aligned activities?
- What could be the obstacles in implementing the Taxonomy?

Bystanders or change makers? Where do management controllers fit in the digital world?

Florence Cavélius, Christoph Endenich, and Adrián Zicari
ESSEC Business School

Brave new (digital) world

'Data is the new gold.'

As inhabitants of a digital world, you've no doubt heard this catchline many times already. And it's true. Although we do not gaze longingly at data in the same way that some do gold in all its shiny allure, the analogy fits. Especially considering the millions of prospectors all over the globe scrambling to get their hands on it.

Data is now the most valuable resource in the world, beating out oil, according to *The Economist*. In these days of the Data Gold Rush, companies find themselves sifting, sorting, and searching through the mountains of digital breadcrumbs we leave behind – video, image, audio, text, sensor, GPS, cell phone, website traffic, and more – in pursuit of meaningful insights and information that can revolutionise their businesses and open the door to a world of new opportunities.

Capturing all the available data – Big Data – is essential to digital transformation efforts. Trying to exploit the strategic business potential embedded in Big Data and, as such, fuel the digital transformation journey, an increasing number of organisations have started to renovate their business models or develop new ones. But that's not enough. Management control systems need a revamp as well. In this light, digital transformation, the 'external' approach towards the market and the consumer, needs ample support 'internally' – through a new approach to management control.

DOI: 10.4324/9781003317333-19

Beyond the boring grey

Historically, management controllers have mostly been dealing with budgeting and reporting. There is an image of controllers that plagues the occupation. That of antisocial number crunchers, locked away in a small office, eyes glued to computer screens.

And that's not the whole story. They are usually described as holding rather passive roles with a relatively low influence on decision-making. This 'traditional' role is also strongly connected with the management controller's focus on consistency and reliability of information inside of the firm.

In order to ensure data reliability, management controllers are often compelled to do tasks such as checking data consistency and eliminating errors. This 'dirty work' can represent a significant share of their work time, leaving them aside from decision-making processes and eventually contributing to the negative image of management controllers as boring beancounters married to Excel.

But 'boring' accounting is a thing of the past. Most information that arises today from Big Data is non-accounting information: companies measure client satisfaction through the tone of customer calls and/or body language, track their clients' holiday destinations, and analyse thousands of reviews, rankings, and ratings in apps and social media. All these data can be used for building a competitive offer, but processing it with Excel will definitely make it crash. New business realities call for new tools.

But before we explore how Big Data is shaping the management accountant's role, let us shine light on the otherwise dark corners of the topic.

The nitty-gritty

The Five V's concept – Volume, Velocity, Variety, Veracity, and Value – gives an idea of the different dimensions through which people approach Big Data.

To begin with, we have volume, which refers to the vast amounts of data generated every second. Just think of all the emails, tweets, photos, video clips, and sensor data we produce and share every second.

Second, velocity is the speed at which new data is generated and the speed at which data moves around. Social media messages go viral in seconds. It takes only milliseconds for trading systems to analyse social media networks and pick up signals that trigger decisions to buy or sell shares.

Next, variety refers to the different types of data we can now use. Data comes in all shapes, sizes, and colours. It can be spreadsheets, or just text documents, videos, and images.

The fourth V is veracity, the quality of the data. Gathered data could have missing pieces, may be inaccurate or may not be able to provide real, valuable insights. For example, data on social media handles could be out of date for a given purpose. Similarly, we have fake news, fabricated reviews, etc.

Last but never least, there is the most important V to take into account when looking at Big Data: value. It is all well and good having access to a tsunami of data but unless we can turn it into value it is useless.

In sum, Big Data is not just about big amounts of information, but about big amounts of 'incoherent' information, coming from countless sources, some of them less trustworthy than others. And so, before drawing any conclusions, it is essential to clean things up. This is exactly where a controller has a card to play.

Make headway

Management controllers, once they have mastered Big Data and new tools, can become actively involved in the ongoing digital transformation, learning from the increasing mass of data, making sense of it, and eventually taking value out of it. As such, the role of controllers evolves from being 'technicians' – that is, people in charge of reporting – to 'business partners': advisors with the power to influence management decisions. In the most digitalised companies, management controllers are at the core of the information process, providing an internal backbone for a long-term transformational shift.

Front or back wagon?

However, transformation in management control practices does not occur everywhere at the same pace. While some management controllers become more involved in consulting and ad hoc missions, others still remain putting debit and credit together in a balance sheet. This is because companies have varying levels of maturity in leveraging Big Data. Accordingly, we can pin down three groups of companies comprising firms with low, middle, and high levels of maturity. Depending on the type, management controllers either play the role of 'technician', similar to traditional accountants, or go the full distance and become an 'augmented business partner'.

Low maturity: Companies that belong to this first group still work in a very traditional way with very limited or no engagement in digital issues.

This behaviour is largely attributed to external factors. For example, in the pharmaceutical industry, margins are comfortable and regulatory constraints prevent digital evolution, such as in advertising. Further, a few companies explain that they are not interested in Big Data because their business models are perceived as not requiring huge amounts of data. As a consequence, their management control systems remain rather conventional, with most resources still snowed under with Excel spreadsheets.

Middle maturity: In this second group, companies have already made an investment in digitalisation, but their transformation is not yet fully achieved. In other words, these companies already have some tools and have begun collecting increasing volumes of data. They are looking beyond Excel to manage the data after realising its limitations of scalability.

This group already addresses the first three V's of Big Data: volume, velocity, and variety. However, one of their most important challenges is the aspect of data veracity. For instance, imagine not getting the same figures from salespeople and controllers. Such issues of consistency may prove to be very hazardous. As such, facing huge amounts of information, these companies are still in search of an optimal way to sieve the available data so that it can serve as a reliable basis for future decisions. Number crunching is not sufficient to generate value from the new data (the fifth V), so the work remains close to a traditional, 'technical' one.

High maturity: Companies in this group have succeeded in becoming digital players and have transformed their business models and introduced new products and services. They now sell clicks. Big Data is used to support decision-making processes and ultimately increase the value of the business. In other words, these companies have successfully reached the Fifth V.

Now freed up from data-reliability missions (the dirty work), management controllers can work on new procedures, for instance, improving routine tasks or revising traditional budgeting processes. As such, they have more time for ad hoc and advisory activities. Instead of struggling with a yearly budget, management controllers establish rolling forecasts which are perceived to be much more responsive to an increasingly volatile business environment. All this helps to make management controllers augmented business partners – able to work more closely with operational units, discuss with managers, or even be a proactive force and propose business solutions.

A helping hand

Obviously, the challenge is particularly high in the early stages of the digital transformation because new tools need to be implemented, new roles need to be defined, and new routines need to be developed.

Having the latest digital technology does not automatically transform manager controllers into business partners. At least, not overnight. Thus, the conversion to this new role needs a collection of empowerment practices, for instance, training sessions and adapted recruitment policies.

No pain, no gain

As data collection and processing become increasingly automatised, the role of management controllers might well diminish, unless they are able to show their capacity to add value in a new digitalised context. Management controllers can do that by going beyond the role of the 'datasmith' – making sense of data, reflecting on business opportunities, and challenging managers with their expert knowledge and judgements.

As such, management controllers can become even more important in decision-making processes, thus becoming 'augmented business partners'. Subsequently, they can play a central role in the successful companies of the digital age.

Key takeaways

- In the digital era, Big Data has become the new gold. An increasing number of firms are transforming their business models – and also face the challenge of transforming management control systems.
- Management controllers, once they have mastered Big Data and new tools, can become actively involved in the digital transformation of their companies, and can add value to the emerging mass of data.
- The role of controllers evolves from being 'technicians' or people in charge of reporting, to 'business partners' – advisors with the power to influence management decisions.
- In most digitalised companies, management controllers are at the heart of information exchange, providing an internal backbone for a long-term transformational shift.
- The reason why transformation in management control practices do not occur everywhere at the same pace is that companies have different maturity levels in leveraging Big Data.

    - Low maturity: Still work in a traditional approach with limited or no engagement in digital issues.
    - Middle maturity: Started to collect huge volumes of data but have not yet leveraged the full potential of digitisation.
    - High maturity: Fully organise Big Data collection, structuring it with powerful tools, in a reliable way.

- Depending on the type, management controllers either play the role of 'technician', similar to traditional accountants, or make a full way to an 'augmented business partner'.

Food for thought

- How has the advent of Big Data impacted accounting tasks/activities in your organisation? What are the skills of accounting professionals operating in the digital era?
- What is the maturity level of your company in leveraging Big Data? What efforts have been undertaken to improve the current level?
- How can your firm ensure that its management accountants move beyond number crunching and elevate their status to strategic and advisory partners?

Why businesses need to account for their climate impacts across the supply chain

Frederik Dahlmann
Warwick Business School

Following the election of US President Joe Biden, things have begun to change. A far cry from ex-President Trump's days when climate change was deemed a hoax and environmental policy shelved. Indeed, firms and organisations, spurred by new interest and initiatives into reducing carbon emissions over recent years, have begun to clean up their footprints. All this spells hope, but to what extent? And what impact? One of the key areas in this attempt to green up operations seems to have gone amiss – that of including supply chains on the spring cleaning list.

Taken for a ride?

Look at the boom in electric scooters, for instance. Both buyers and promotors of the machines have long claimed the electric scooter as an ecofriendly way of travelling city distances. As such, every day we can witness the number of Uber and Grab employees using the bigger machines, while we dodge office workers and students buzzing about on the leaner, trendier machines.

Nevertheless, the majority of electric scooter manufacturers are Chinese firms, and most of them omit to keep a record of their carbon footprint. In addition, due to a non-durable design and build, many scooters never in fact live out an efficient life cycle. Taken from this angle, the popularity of the electric scooter has ridden to popularity on a single slice of the life-cycle pie that is lenient on emissions – that of actually riding it. But research carried out on the whole chain of operations in a dockless scooter's life – from raw materials, manufacturing, and distribution to transportation, maintenance, upkeep, and disposal at the end of its use – reveals that the ticket to ride is far less green than the makers would like us to believe.

DOI: 10.4324/9781003317333-20

Engagement – not enough but getting there

Not giving the supply chain enough attention is not good news for the environment. Indeed, it is these that can amount to the main culprit in an organisation's carbon emissions – on average up to 11.4 times the quantity of companies' own emissions stem from operations. Moreover, few companies seem aware of how much they pollute from their supply chains. However, there is some progress in sensitising firms, notably through a charity going under the name of *The Carbon Disclosure Project (CDP)* which conducts an annual survey of companies. The results of this survey point to an increased engagement from companies and their suppliers, with 75% of suppliers surveyed now disclosing their scope 1 and 2 emissions. However, many suppliers remain initially hesitant to make such data public and do not account for their own scope 3 emissions.

This is disquieting on two fronts. Firstly, because regulation is supposed to put a choke on non-disclosure of emissions, regulators around the globe request publicly listed companies to come clean with their greenhouse gas (GHG) emission numbers and make them public in their annual reports. One such country is the United Kingdom which effectively subjects the whole supply chain to scrutiny. Secondly, thanks to activists like Greta Thunberg, climate change has become a top concern for the wider public and politicians the world over, with pressure building for firms to clean up their act – not simply using their reductions in emissions for positive image via the media, but, crucially, for leading business and society to a greener, sustainable future. In this light, it is increasingly important for firms to tackle – and involve themselves with – the various stakeholders in their supply chains to work together towards drastically reducing carbon emissions.

Three levels of focus in supply chains

Research on the CDP surveys for the period 2014–2017 covers 1,686 listed companies worldwide which actively collect environmental data and engage with their supply chain end to end – from suppliers to customers. Analysis of this data points to only 28% of these firms engaging with customers, while a lowly 21% engage with their suppliers. The remaining 51% of firms discuss with both ends of their supply chain. For companies overall, however, a hefty two-thirds of them do neither, although during the period in question it must be noted that a 57% increase in engagement with part or all of their supply chain was recorded.

From this data, it is possible to place firms into three different categories based on their level of involvement with the supply chain: basic, transactional, and collaborative with the collaborative stage often entailing the most all-inclusive approach of engagement with suppliers, customers, and other partners.

At the basic level, firms typically request their suppliers to fill out a survey on their emissions data. Examples include US software firm Symantec which produces an annual report on its suppliers' GHG emissions, and the Bank of America which has been running a CDP supply chain survey since 2009. However, firms at this stage typically measure and assemble data and, as such, commit to only the first step required for the design of a fuller, more effective carbon reduction plan. It is worth noting that emissions reports from companies committing to only basic engagement were shorter in length and less detailed in qualitative terms. On another footing, companies at the transactional or collaborative levels use the data more proactively, for instance to estimate their carbon footprint and find opportunities for improvements.

The more experienced and committed firms of those studied seem to use the data to set targets and incentives for their supply chain. That is the case in the instance of Virgin Atlantic Airways and nuclear power firm Exelon. In addition, this data is also employed for the development of KPIs which can be used for supplier selection and the assessment of their performance.

As part of the continuous process, firms failing to hit requisite performance levels are issued with warnings and improvements demanded. As such, emissions data becomes an integral part of the selection criteria for suppliers and makes them more accountable. Pharma giant Pfizer, for instance, uses that data to provide benchmarks for its suppliers.

Working on the chain

At the collaborative level, firms and suppliers work together to develop shared goals: collaboration is more tightly knit. In order to build beneficial, win–win, and greener relationships aimed at reducing overall carbon footprint, a deeper involvement and commitment is necessary from firms and suppliers that call for more meetings, seminars on sharing best practice, and more personal interactions in the form of phone calls and emails including the establishment of online discussion groups. Some firms also offer supportive supplier training and development courses, briefings, summits, and award ceremonies with the aim of pinpointing the potential for joint development of innovation projects.

At the other end of the chain, firms at the collaborative level work together with their clients, persuading them about the benefits of greener products and the need to use those products in a way that is less harmful to the planet.

Indeed, companies bring the collaborative relationship to life in a variety of different ways. Food giant Kellogg's, for example, has created a 'Sustainability Consortium' with its supply chain, while the InterContinental Hotels Group works with the International Tourism Partnership to diminish the environmental impact of its bed linen. Moreover, Sodexo, the French hospitality and catering firm, partners with associations and academia, for example with Euromed Management (now Kedge) in Marseilles. Furthermore, some companies use both transactional and collaborative modes of engagement at the same time with many stakeholders.

At the end of the day, calculating carbon emissions across the life cycle of a product – from sourcing raw materials to the final product ending up in a landfill – is no easy task. Moreover, it underlines the increasing importance of a collaborative approach. The requirement for companies to report their emissions makes them more accountable in a system where what you do necessarily impacts the rest. As such, it is crucial for firms to understand that they are part of a single system that must work together, rather than simply employing emissions monitoring as a supply chain management tool.

The role of data

The importance of data should be kept in mind, for tracking emissions can be extremely complex especially for the likes of food distribution firms such as Walmart. Given the amount of data to crunch, it comes as no surprise that tech companies are leading the way in the reduction of their carbon footprints. Their inherent data analytics skills serve not only to collect data but for them to use this data effectively upwards and downwards throughout the supply chain. Besides having an advantage, tech companies are likely to be in a perfect position to be able to develop emissions management platforms and tech that is much in demand – especially given the increasing requirement for emissions accounting.

New market openings are on the offer if tech companies are able to resolve the complex puzzle of supply chains and produce a comprehensive software package that does it all – track, record, and manage carbon emission across the entire chain. Verizon, among others, for example, sees its IoT products, designed to reduce carbon emissions, as 'providing significant revenue opportunities'.

It is clear that sustainability will be the issue of the younger generation, which is engaged as never before in the fight for climate change. If businesses are to prosper in this context, they need to look at sustainability in their whole supply chain. And this, not only to avoid being accused of artistic carbon accounting, but also to legitimately claim that they are truly on the planet's side.

Key takeaways

- Despite firms' growing attempts to green up their operations, they have to large extent overlooked their supply chains.
- Supply chains can be the biggest contributor to a firm's carbon emissions – on average 11.4 times the quantity of its own emissions stemming from operations. Few companies seem aware.
- Research based on CDP survey data from 2017 covering 1,686 listed companies worldwide identified 28% of firms engaging with customers, while 21% engage with their suppliers and 51% of firms exchange data and information with both ends of their supply chain. Overall, two-thirds of companies do neither. However, between 2014 and 2019, there was a 57% increase in engagement with part or all of their supply chain.
- Firms surveyed by the CDP tend to engage with supply chain partners through three main types of approaches: basic, transactional, and collaborative.
- At the basic level, firms typically request their suppliers to fill out a survey on their emissions data but do very little with that information.
- At the transactional level, firms use these data to calculate their complete scopes 1–3 carbon footprints and identify opportunities for improvements.
- They use the data to manage their supply chain partners with targets, incentives, and KPIs during supplier selection and performance assessment processes.
- At the collaborative level, firms understand that they are part of a single system that must work together, rather than simply employing emissions monitoring as a supply chain management tool.
- Collaborative forms of engagement are used to develop novel processes for greenhouse gas emissions reductions across the whole supply chain (including customers and suppliers).
- Firms use collaborative engagement to support, educate, and steer supply chain partners towards collective emissions reduction initiative through significant product and process innovation.

• Many tech firms are leading in this area as their data-driven business models provide them with an advantage and opportunity to develop all-in-one supply chain software to help combat carbon emissions.

Food for thought

• Think of your firm or organisation. To what extent is it transparent on its own carbon footprint? And to what extent do you feel pressure to act and reduce your emissions?
• To what extent do you account for scope 3 emissions – all those generated by suppliers during the production stages as well as those generated by customers during the use phase?
• Who are your company's/organisation's stakeholders – and how might you engage with them in collaborative efforts to become greener?
• Which three areas of your firm's/organisation's activities would you most concentrate on to lower negative environmental effects? What initiatives or projects would you launch? And what would be their objectives?

Related works:

– *How to manage your supply chain's carbon footprint*, Frederik Dahlmann, Warwick CORE Insights, January 2020.
– *How to really hold business to account on their carbon footprint – include their supply chains*, Frederik Dahlmann, The Conversation, January 2020.

Micro case study 1: Accounting

SuperSuper, part 1

You are a member of the board of SuperSuper, a large chain of supermarkets with operations all over Europe and Latin America. You are the only board member who is not a family member. The company was founded by John Super in the early 50s, and remains controlled by the family of the founder. However, the company is quoted in a major stock exchange where a sizeable part of the shares is held by many investors. The company has long been considered a reliable investment by financial analysts and the specialized press. Here is an excerpt from the board discussion.

Paul Super: I am tired of these minority shareholders! You know what some of them are asking? That we prepare a sustainability report. We have more important things to do!

Peter Super: Well, this is a trend that is spreading fast. Most of our competitors are doing that now.

Patrick Super: It remains challenging for us. You know, we have a good accounting system, but dealing with non-financial information – that's another story. We'd need to collect, record, and track information about different units of measure – I mean hours, tons of materials, people, and so on and data which isn't currently even in our accounting system. Setting up a reasonably good, reliable system for that data is far from being a minor investment.

Paul Super: Luckily, there are no legal obligations. Most of these disclosures are voluntary.

Peter Super: Not that fast! Indeed, some countries where we operate have been implementing regulations. But not in all of them, I concede. In Europe, there is Directive 2014/95/EU that asks for some disclosures. Then, we have 'soft-law' initiatives – for instance, the GRI (Global Reporting Initiative).

Pamela Super: In any case, I remain hesitant. Our competitors will gain more information about us – that's uncomfortable. Why should we spend money in this kind of reporting?

Merely to please a few shareholders? They can sell their shares and that's it!

Peter Super: Precisely, that is the point. Some shareholders may like our move and remain loyal investors. Maybe even accompany us further in our next public offer! Then, we have clients.

Pamela Super: Come on! Clients *don't* read our reports before buying . . . or maybe they do. But I imagine that a company that regularly publishes a sustainability report becomes more appreciated.

Paul Super: Perhaps these minority shareholders are not so wrong after all. You know? We should meet some of them.

And you, the only board member who is not a Super, what do you think? Should SuperSuper present sustainability reports? Which are the potential benefits? Which are the potential risks?

Micro case study 2: Accounting

SuperSuper, part 2

After much discussion, SuperSuper implemented several social accounting tools and drafted its first sustainability report. Now you are a strategy consultant working with the company board. You have a meeting with one of the directors, Pamela Super, who is also the CFO.

> **Pamela Super:** Our sustainability report is nice. So nice that we got a prize for it! But in practice, we don't get much value out of it. For us, social accounting and conventional accounting are two different worlds.
>
> **You:** It's true that both kinds of reports have different scopes and objectives. But interactions still exist. Take an investment to improve environmental performance. This will appear in the Profit and Loss statement, of course. At the same time, the improvement in environmental performance will appear – hopefully – in the sustainability report.
>
> **Pamela Super:** Okay, but these are two different audiences. Whoever reads the P&L does not read the sustainability report. And vice versa.
>
> **You:** This used to be the case for a long time, I concede. But nowadays some investors are beginning to take a glance at the sustainability report. At least, to better grasp the company's long-term risks.
>
> **Pamela Super:** In any case, preparing a sustainability report doesn't make our company better. We may learn a few things in the process, and that's fine. But reporting in itself doesn't improve our operations.
>
> **You:** Yes, but as you well say – you learn during the process. You understand better some of your risks, and you get a better sense of where you are compared to your competitors who also report.
>
> **Pamela Super:** Would you please prepare a short report for us explaining the use of sustainability reports? How can we better learn from them? While we prepare them, and while we read them afterwards. And how can we tell our investors that it makes sense to read our sustainability report as attentively as they read our financial reports?

4 The accounting profession

Ethics, influence, and conduct

For better or for worse? The special ties between accounting firms and their clients – influence and behaviours

Qinqin Zheng
School of Management Fudan University

A strategic and trusting partnership

Legally required to produce financial statements, pay taxes, and produce regular audit reports, it comes as no surprise to learn that every company in every industry has accounting needs. In today's business world, a partnership with an accounting firm is an absolute necessity, and more often than not they become very special business partners for their client companies.

Moreover, an accounting firm can be much more than a simple bookkeeper. Accounting service is knowledge-intensive and highly professional, the job involving access to a firm's confidential business information and diving into internal processes. Despite the fact that the IFRS or GAAP provide specific guidelines and requirements, every firm is unique in its organisational structure and approach to business activities, rendering a 'one-size-fits-all' approach inapplicable. In short, the opinions and solutions provided by accounting firms are necessarily highly customised and specifically aimed at their clients' needs and requirements.

As such, since a solution cannot be offered to another client, it's in a service provider's interest to maintain close ties with the client. On the client side, giving access to highly sensitive and confidential information means that they are also interested in building a long-term relationship with a reliable service provider. Mutual benefits thereby transform the standard provider–customer relationship into meaningful business partnerships.

The complexity of a relationship

Positioned as a strategic partner rather than an ordinary professional service provider, an accounting firm is what psychology calls 'an important other' – people in one's sphere who have an important impact. And in

DOI: 10.4324/9781003317333-22

its role as a long-term business partner, an accounting firm becomes an 'important other' that might affect clients' moral conduct and behaviours.

Moreover, the relationship between partners becomes much more complex and uncertain when it comes to ethical issues, for as clients and accounting firms form a kind of joint venture, any immoral activity will put both parties at risk. In terms of ethics, clients are often considered 'first movers', unintentionally or not providing incorrect or biased information – with the accounting firm becoming involved, despite itself, in the client's possible immoral conduct. Let's take an example: auditors, for instance, might be encouraged to issue an unqualified opinion regarding a financial statement. This poses a dilemma, for as a service provider, an accounting firm will try its hardest to satisfy its clients' needs, while also trying its hardest to stick to the expert and ethical attributes of its profession.

Things get more intriguing still. For being a partner and not a subordinate, an accounting firm may wield a non-negligible measure of influence on its client. Faced with their clients' unethical conduct, this influence can come in three forms – positive influence, no influence, or negative influence.

In theory, accounting firms should stick to strict moral principles. In practice, it is more complex. Accounting firms can be reluctant to be too tough – the risk being that they might lose the client. But going down this road carries with it the risk of taking undue advantage of the situation or collusions in misconduct leading to potentially explosive media coverage if discovered.

The truth always gets out in the end goes the old adage – and it is true of accounting scandals too, most of them occurring when auditors choose to remain silent when confronted with a client's immoral conduct or even lend support to it. No need to look far for an example, as almost every large accounting firm has found itself under scrutiny at one point or another. KPMG in 2003, for instance, was found jointly responsible (although not sanctioned) for misconduct in the Jinzhou Port case, falsifying financial statements to woo investors. Two years later, a similar issue shrouded Deloitte Touche Tohmatsu. Despite possessing codes of ethics and conduct, accounting firms may still exert negative influence, albeit perhaps indirectly in some circumstances, on their clients if they fail to oppose unethical business practices.

Consciously unaware in China

As with any relationship, discussions between accounting firms and their clients do not always go smoothly. In industrial tribunal cases – or worse still, the criminal court – misdemeanor can often lead to both sides hurling accusations at each other in an attempt to prove greater or lesser levels of guilt. But in China, there is a 'failure to notice immoral behaviour' clause – a common excuse for accounting firms to be left off the hook or punished gently in corporate scandals after submitting the excuse of incapability of awareness. In the cases of KPMG and Deloitte, for example, no substantial punishment has yet been issued by the Chinese government to these accounting firms.

Auditor firms, who are supposed to interact closely with their clients, are also supposed to be responsible for the service provided – and thoroughly capable of identifying corporate moral hazard. Indeed, it is an inherent part of their job – and challenges their professionalism if not undertaken correctly.

Research carried out on 1,000+ Chinese listed companies and 65 accounting firms in a seven-year period seems to prove the point. The results are coherent with the viewpoint of the CSRC (China Securities Regulatory Commission) regarding breaches of conduct, implying that accounting firms *do* have the basic capabilities to identify ethical issues in corporate information disclosure. Furthermore, much higher hazard rates were observed for qualified opinion than for unqualified, meaning that when an accounting firm identifies any problems with information disclosure, the company under scrutiny can almost be sure to have an underlying ethics issue.

Field for action

Back to the code of ethics – a must-have for the market. In the case of accounting firms, the Generally Accepted Accounting Principles (GAAP) on independence, integrity, and objectivity have been adopted. However, these codes do not go beyond self-regulation. They require accounting firms to be guided by ethical principles in their activities, but this is where the area of their responsibility ends. However, given these firms' power of influence and their special status, would it not be reasonable to expect them to also ethically influence their client companies?

Moreover, in their position as 'important others', accounting firms should logically have ethical obligations to positively influence their clients. This leads to the argument that incapability of awareness of a client's immoral conduct is simply unsubstantiated. As such, denying any responsibility compromises the highly professional image of an accounting firm. After all, true professionals should hold responsibility for the results of their work – for if denied, can they still be called professional?

In this light, it has been suggested that accounting firms should make greater effort to exercise positive influence on their clients. Yet this is easier said than done. It is becoming increasingly challenging for auditors to persuade their clients of the necessity to abide by moral codes, especially if their client faces financial difficulties. For example, in China, regulations on the stock market stipulate that if a listed company reports losses over three consecutive years, it will be the subject of 'special treatment' and face the risk of being delisted. Likewise, if a listed company remains in negative cash flow for two years running, it also indicates negative performance with the company facing the need to refinance for more cash. More often than not, companies faced with such situations will try their hardest to keep the sinking ship afloat. And the high motivation to survive carries with it the temptation to resort to misinformation or cooking the books – along with greater effort to persuade their accounting partners to help them stay above water through a qualified audit report.

The bigger they are, the bigger the temptation?

Every company has an interest in being a good one. And it is fair to say that it is not the relationship itself but other factors that come into play to increase the corporate moral hazard rate. The financial shape of a company is one of them, but there are others too – for example, the duration of the client-accounting firm relationship – the longer the duration, the lower the risk of straying from the path. Research has found that the moral hazard rate dropped by a healthy 19%.

On the other hand, some factors turn out to be less important than expected. Size, for example. Would a Big Four firm do a better job in preventing immoral behaviour than a small- or medium-sized audit firm? One would tend to lean towards the yes – logically, a large, international accounting firm with higher qualifications and stronger capabilities would gain greater trust. Moreover, this was exactly the logic applied when in 2001 – in order to reduce the rate of business scandals – the CSRC issued its *Rule Sixteen* compelling listed companies to recruit international accounting firms for their audit needs. Since then, however, there has been no statistical evidence to support the claim that large firms such as the Big Four demonstrate better performance in transmitting ethical conduct to their clients. Indeed, some are now calling for *Rule Sixteen* to be discarded.

What about changing accounting firms regularly? Here again, research has shown no significant effect on reducing the probability of immoral conduct when a company changes its auditor. And this despite the logic that a new relationship necessarily fosters renewed care in firms providing accurate information, or the auditor being more vigilant on any ethical issues.

All in all, the moral dialogue between audit firms and their clients still has a long way to go, with a quantity of external and internal factors influencing such a special relationship. On the other hand, an important conclusion is that audit firms *do* have the power to influence corporate clients. And they *do* have the power to influence them positively and to encourage them to act in a moral and ethical way. The fact that the task is challenging does not mean that there is no hope for a happy ending for the couple. Long-term relationships between accounting firms and their clients can actually facilitate interactions and enhance mutual understanding. And the longer the relationship, the easier it is for accounting firms to share ethical codes with their clients. The most important thing, after all, is to keep on trying.

Key takeaways

- An accounting firm is a special business partner for a client company. The former proposes costly customised solutions while the latter needs a reliable long-term partner. Mutual benefits transform the provider–customer relationship between firms and their clients into meaningful business partnerships.
- Given the special status of accounting firms and access to confidential information, auditors have influence over their clients. Through their attitude and actions, accounting firms may either improve or worsen the moral qualities of their clients.
- Accounting firms can be reluctant to be too tough with clients in the case of an ethical issue for fear of losing them, with the risk of getting involved in opportunisms or collusions.
- In China, when accounting firms find themselves caught up in corporate scandals, they may deny shared responsibility under the 'incapability of awareness' clause. However, auditor firms who interact with clients so closely, and who adhere to a set of professional principles and working methods, cannot be completely unaware of moral hazards.
- Given their power of influence, special status, and knowledge of client companies, accounting firms should undertake ethical obligations to positively influence clients. All of them are equal: no evidence suggests that large international accounting firms will succeed more than smaller ones.
- The longer the relationship, the easier it is to find a right approach, while a firm's financial difficulties increase moral hazard rates.

Food for thought

- To what extent do you think there is a limit to moral conduct between friends, couples, or partners? Is there naturally a 'breaking point' where one or the other in a relationship strays from the path? Why would it be different between professionals and working partners?

- What professions would you list that require strict, moral guidelines and laws and regulations to provide a framework to avoid unethical behaviour?
- In the case of China in the aforementioned text, what advice and recommendations would you offer the government and the CSRC regarding the auditor–client working relationship?

Related research: *The Influence of Accounting Firms on Clients' Immoral Behaviors in China, Journal of Business Ethics Vol. 91, Supplement 1: THE 2ND WORLD BUSINESS ETHICS FORUM THEME: RETHINKING THE VALUE OF BUSINESS ETHICS (2010), Springer*

From lobby to the audit office

Big Four accounting firms and political links

Anastasios Elemes and Jeff Zeyun Chen
ESSEC Business School
Neeley School of Business, Texas Christian University

The importance of politics

Politicians may not be the apple of the public eye. They may not – as the latest Edelman Trust Barometer indicates – earn the public's trust. But politicians and governments are useful for companies. These companies include the likes of accounting firms such as EY, Deloitte, KPMG, and PwC – the Big Four. Indeed, these firms' political connections at a national level can be put to good effect in lobbying for shaping accounting and auditing standards – and also for their clients' interests too.

It would be tempting to conclude that such relationships might compromise the auditing firm's independence and, possibly, their moral behaviour. For it is rare for help in any form not to contain a trade-off or, more positively put, a win–win: *I do this for you, so you do this for me*. Natural, no?

Moreover, it also might seem natural to accept that large corporations indeed donate to political parties. In some countries – those that haven't banned such donations – this is tightly regulated with ceilings on corporate donations set by law. In others, the system is more lenient for national-level donations. But what might be surprising is that accounting firms lobby at local level too – through their offices and subsidiaries and through their donations. So what impact does this local financial contribution have? Let's take a closer look.

Home-grown

Large accounting firms – the Big Four – are widely respected for their professionalism and their role in ensuring the independent credibility of financial reports. They are also constantly monitored by the SEC and the PCAOB in order to uphold rigorous and ethical conduct in their business dealings. Not to mention their own sets of Codes of Ethics. Yet, these have not prevented the Big Four headquarters from significantly increasing their

DOI: 10.4324/9781003317333-23

political action committee (PAC) donations in recent years. And in addition to the national level, studies have shown the employees of the Big Four to have sent campaign money directly to members of the congressional committees who supervise the auditing industry.

Prior studies having looked into the national level, we have focused – retrieving auditor connections data from the period 2003–2012 – on the local dimension to understand auditors' political connections at the office level and in order to gauge if these links have an impact on audit behaviours and quality through analysing earnings restatements. Local donations make sense because the congress members who legislate are themselves geographically dispersed throughout the US and necessarily match the presence of auditing offices throughout the country.

The expected pros and cons of political connections

An immediate reaction might be that anything a firm has to do with politics naturally influences – and negatively so – how that firm acts. Previous research has indeed found evidence that points in this direction. Firms, it argues, having connections to political parties, will benefit from less scrutiny and therefore more leeway in terms of the quality of service provided. This is especially so if audit firms have special ties with regulatory bodies, with lower odds of being inspected and lower penalties for audits if they go askew. And because an auditing firm has close connections, bound by donations, it would have a lower incentive for producing top-quality work than if the firm were not linked through political connections.

But all is not negative. Indeed, one of the key benefits of having special relations with the politicians and the authorities is that audit firms can provide excellent information and expertise to the former for improvements to policies and regulations. This may take the form of lobbying, for sure – but it also means that to be listened, the credibility and reputation of an auditor count. The Big Four are in such a position to offer that. Moreover, a counter argument would be that quality would be maintained, if not heightened, because any straying from the path would put their reputations and political links at risk. It's therefore in an audit firm's interest to keep up the standard – and keep to good conduct.

Finally, ties between the Big Four and politicians go deep and wide, a chunky 57% of politicians targeted during the 2003–2012 period occurring at both national and office levels. It is also interesting to note that this lobbying intensifies during periods when regulations are being developed and set – for example, in 2003–2004, when the Sarbanes-Oxley act was implemented, and again in 2007, to support the presidential campaign of

Chris Dodd, the then chairman of the Senate's banking, housing, and urban affairs committee.

That nagging question of quality – a final check

So the argument goes that political connections at the level of the auditor office might negatively affect the quality of an audit firm's work. But to check this over time, we decided to look into the frequency of earnings restatements – that is, when a P&L statement is changed or rectified because mistakes in auditing have been identified. Results seem to show that the tendency to restate earnings is not in fact linked to audit office political connections. Moreover, when litigation risk is higher, the higher the audit quality – because politically connected audit firms are placed under greater scrutiny both by the regulators and also the public. Subsequently, audit firms reduce risk to a minimum by upping the quality of their work. Auditor political links therefore have an effect of increasing the quality of audit and not decreasing it.

When given the close ties and relationships between auditors and their clients, a degree of overlook, tolerance, or bending of the rules might come into play. But here too, research at the local level points towards audit firms sticking to rules of conduct without resorting to 'flexibility'.

And finally, a twist in the tale might be that while fewer restatements mean better quality, they might also mean that misstatements are not detected or disclosed. And here, research points to that not being the case with politically connected firms having an incentive to reduce the risk of controversy and maintain their reputations by improving disclosure.

However, one dimension on which political links do seem to have an impact is the auditor's independence. During the financial crisis, for example, audits were lighter in nature – and less onerous to the client – in spite of the greater risk of misstatement due to their clients' decrease in profits and potential to inflate the value of their assets. Our findings endorse that. Politically connected auditors tend to lessen their vigilance during years that are subsequently restated. As such, donations seem to imply a negative trade-off – influence for a degree of leeway.

Generally, it seems that while auditors with political ties have an incentive to maintain credibility by delivering quality audits, they are less likely to maintain the same level of audit quality for their connected clients. The close, long-term relationships between auditor and client might have something to do with this. But where there is trust and emotional commitment, a certain level of flexibility might be considered acceptable. And on the lobbying side, as long as conflict of interest or gross misconduct is avoided, some countries will continue to tolerate the system of political donations.

Key takeaways

- Large accounting firms – the Big Four – are widely respected for their professionalism and their role in ensuring the independent credibility of financial reports.
- They are monitored by government enforcement agencies such as the SEC and PCAOB to uphold a rigorous and ethical behaviour in their business dealings.
- But the Big Four donate through their political action committees at a national level, at a local level through their offices, and on an individual basis. The goal is to influence and lobby senators and regulators while providing these with information to shape policies and regulations.
- Lobbying intensifies during periods when regulations are being developed.
- Firms having connections to political parties will benefit from less scrutiny and lower penalties for non-quality.
- However, given the risk to reputation and credibility, the Big Four are likely to maintain quality.
- Research into the frequency of earnings restatements show that, on average, earnings restatements drop with audit office political connections.
- When litigation risk is higher, the higher the audit quality – because politically connected audit firms are placed under greater scrutiny both by the regulators and also the public.
- On average, auditor political links therefore have an effect of increasing the quality of audit and not decreasing it.
- One dimension on which political links do seem to have an impact is the auditor's independence, with lighter and less onerous audits taking place for clients themselves politically connected.

Food for thought

- To what extent would you forbid auditing firms to donate to political parties? Why? And to what extent is there a possible middle ground?
- In an imperfect world, is it only natural for 'trade-offs' to occur in terms of return of favour between audit firms and politicians? What would constitute a red line in terms of favour?
- Imagine you have a savings account and insurance policy with an insurance company. You learn that, during the current election campaign, the company donates to a political party that is far from your own political beliefs. What do you do? And why?

Related research: *Big 4 Office Political Connections and Client Restatements, December 2020, European Accounting Review, DOI: 10.1080/09638180.2020.1856163*

Micro case study 3: Accounting

SuperSuper, part 3

Peter Super, the Chief Accountant of SuperSuper, has a conversation with his brother, Patrick Super, who is now the sustainability manager.

Peter: You, Patrick, all the time making investments in sustainability. But I don't see the results!

Patrick: You know, the path to sustainability isn't that easy. Even in our case. After some initial hesitation, our family became fully convinced and now we have a mandate for implementing sustainability.

Peter: Yes, all over the company, and with a generous budget for that. And you managed to convince the most recalcitrant members of our family!

Patrick: Well, that's the past. The point is that even with full support, with total conviction, we are not fully there yet. I've been thinking a lot about this. And you know? There is some issue with indicators.

Peter: Indicators?

Patrick: Yes. We have a great sustainability report – remember, we got a prize for it. But I wonder if we are that good at analyzing and eventually putting that information to use.

Peter: You mean a disconnection?

Patrick: Indeed, a disconnection between our sustainability reporting – you see the good people that work with me – and the rest of the company. Normally, we pester local managers to collect data for our report, and then, we don't come back to them. In any case, it doesn't work the other way around. I don't remember an intermediate manager asking for any information from us.

Peter: You have a point. Our managers have several indicators and several objectives. None of them is related to sustainability.

Patrick: We know that it's not what we think, but somebody may say that our report is a kind of compliance tool. We tick the box, we have a sustainability report as any other respectable company in our sector, and that's all.

What do you think? Which advice could you give to Peter and Patrick?

Auditing the auditors

How do audit firms manage their own tax affairs?

Anastasios Elemes
ESSEC Business School

Large accounting firms are often credited with the creation of the artificial structures associated with the aggressive tax avoidance of their corporate clients. And there have been many studies, rightfully so, to investigate the accounting and tax practices of these big corporations.

However, it is curious to note that the Big 4 auditing firms – Deloitte, PwC, Ernst & Young, and KPMG – are also big corporations, and there have rarely been any insights and research on how the auditing firms approach their own tax affairs.

Income shifting

Income shifting is the process of redirecting a stream of your revenue to another person, firm, or entity to benefit from tax reductions. As with a lot of regulations concerning taxes, this may sound morally ambiguous but is not illegal. Wealthy individuals and big corporations have been using this tactic for a long time.

There are various ways to practice income shifting such as hiring a family member and claiming their salary as a business deduction, transferring income-producing assets to another taxpayer, and deferring bonuses and income if you expect the income to be less next year so that you don't have to move to the higher tax bracket.

Income shifting in the Big 4

It is essential to understand and inspect the income-shifting activities of accountancy firms themselves for two main reasons. Firstly, these firms are major economic entities in their own right whose activities and practices need to be more transparent so that their impact on society can be better understood. The opacity of such firms is ironic since their core services are centred on accountability and transparency.

DOI: 10.4324/9781003317333-24

Also, the international footprint of the big accounting firms mirrors that of the large multinational groups that are being audited. Thus, the extrapolation of how the Big 4 approach their tax planning, both at the regional and international levels, to how they approach the tax planning services of their clients with multinational operations seems logical.

Big 4 organisational structure

Big 4 firms are similar to law firms in that each firm is independent, while belonging to an international network. At the same time, each firm has to abide with global quality standards, which apply throughout the network. Member firms are not subsidiaries or branch offices of a global parent rather they are separate locally formed legal entities.

Even though Big 4 firms have strong international presence, just like their corporate clients, their organisational structure is often significantly different to that of their multinational clients. Differently from their multinational clients, the regional offices of the Big 4, are in fact different legal entities with local operations. Such decentralisation makes inter-organisational cooperation difficult and hence acts as a deterrent for income shifting in the Big 4 firms.

Apart from the organisational structure, there is another strong disincentive for the Big 4 firms to avoid income shifting: political costs. Regulators are able to impose costs on Big 4 networks if they perceive them as aggressive tax avoiders. They can do that by increasing the scrutiny of Big 4 networks – as well as of their client's tax affairs – and/or limiting their ability to cross-sell tax, advisory, and audit services.

Where there is a will, there is a way

Even with the challenges mentioned earlier, the Big 4 have access to many income-shifting opportunities. They also have in-house expertise on how to optimally structure operations from a tax standpoint and on how to design partner compensation so that outbound income-shifting partners are not disadvantaged. Where there is a will, there is a way, indeed.

While the Big 4 can't deliberately be expected to engage in illegal tax evasion, current freedom and flexibility in setting prices, and in determining the appropriate mix between equity and debt, the appropriateness of some income-shifting strategies becomes a matter of subjective judgement rather than objective truth.

Current income shifting exists in Big 4 networks and often relates to transfer pricing for intra-network transfers of intellectual methodology, brand name, and data analysis tools. And since there is little to no involvement of regulators in determining the prices for such services, the Big 4 networks enjoy complete freedom to fix prices to their convenience.

In addition, the vast geographic dispersion of the Big 4 – which includes a significant presence in tax havens – provides them with ample opportunity for income shifting. Furthermore, with their expertise in guiding multinational clients to structure their operations optimally from a geographic point of view to take advantage of the local tax laws, they can extrapolate the same to their structure.

Profit pooling as a means of income shifting

It is common practice among the Big 4 *'to pool a portion of the revenue from each member firm of a network to focus on initiatives that no member firm can do alone'*. Our research offers a concrete example of how this profit pooling combined with partnerships with local entities provides an opportunity for income shifting.

PricewaterhouseCoopers EE Holdings B.V. is a European coordinating entity of the PwC network. Unsurprisingly, the directors of these entities are also typically partners of the local member firms that participate in the profit-pooling agreements. From the financial statements, the directors of these entities received approximately $13.4 million as remuneration for their services that year.

The example offers evidence that partner involvement in the activities of coordinating entities provides opportunities to structure partner compensation in such a way that it is a convenient and legal means of income shifting. Despite the evidence, current and previous Big 4 partners reveal that cross-border activities are primarily motivated by strategic objectives, not for tax optimisation ones.

With great power comes great responsibility

To be called the Big 4 in any field, you should be very powerful in that field. And the Big 4 in accounting are some of the most powerful firms in the world, their clientele consist of some of the largest organisations. They are omnipresent and exercise their control over firms, business people, politicians, and governments.

With such power comes a great deal of freedom and responsibility. When they can find loopholes to engage in questionable practices, it sets a dangerous precedent for their biggest clients. If they are not careful, as by rule they often are, such practices could lead to their downfall.

Key takeaways

- Auditing firms, through their independent and unbiased work, play a critical role in ensuring that big corporations comply with all applicable laws and regulations.
- Income shifting is the process of redirecting a stream of your revenue to another person, firm, or entity to benefit from tax reductions.
- The extrapolation of how the Big 4 approach their tax planning, both at the regional and international levels, to how they approach the tax planning services of their clients with multinational operations seems logical.
- The Big 4 have access to many income-shifting opportunities as well as the in house expertise on how to optimally structure operations from a tax standpoint. They also know how to design partner compensation so that outbound income-shifting partners are not disadvantaged even in the absence of formal cross-border integration.
- The vast geographic dispersion of the Big 4 which includes a significant presence in tax havens provides them with ample opportunity for income shifting.
- It is common practice among the Big 4 *'to pool a portion of the revenue from each member firm of a network to focus on initiatives that no member firm can do alone'*. This money is distributed at the discretion of the firm.
- When the Big 4 can find loopholes to engage in questionable practices, it sets a dangerous precedent for their biggest clients.

Food for thought

- To what extent do firms have a moral obligation to pay taxes?
- Should there be a special rule regarding accounting firms given their role as upholders of the law?
- If you, in your current position or future career, were asked to find a 'creative solution' to lower tax payments, how would you react? What would make you do it and what would make you want to avoid it? How many points does each question score?

Related research: *Tax-motivated Profit Shifting in Big 4 Networks: Evidence From Europe, May 2021, Accounting Organizations and Society, DOI: 10.1016/j.aos.2021.101267*

Walk the talk

How firms gain environmental legitimacy

Liliana Gelabert
IE Business School

Tough call

Firms need environmental legitimacy. In an era of growing environmental concerns, it is crucial for them to demonstrate to investors, clients, employees, and society at large that you care about creating long-term value. Indeed, on an external level, various groups of stakeholders – from customers to local communities and NGOs – seek to make sure that sustainable development goals are not an empty barrel for corporate leaders, with ESG (Environmental, Social, and Governance) performance expected to be at the top of the corporate agenda. Added to that, environmental legitimacy is becoming a key competitive factor, while acquiring this legitimacy is fast becoming a major strategic concern.

There are many ways in which firms can publicly communicate their positive environmental intentions, but some of them seem to produce better results than others. In this context, 'better' implies that they correspond more to external expectations and therefore help firms to gain stronger legitimacy.

Which actions and policies are more efficient for gaining credibility? Some actions undertaken by companies cost more to implement than others. And while little is known about the real motivations behind corporate decisions to go green, more information is available on how many resources are required to put these decisions into practice. This provides a clue on how we can distinguish between efficient signals and less efficient ones.

Seeing is believing

It can be very challenging for the general public or non-specialised investors to assess a firm's environmental footprint as most people lack knowledge of the real environmental quality of the firm's production processes. But there are two key features that help identify stronger signals of environmental

DOI: 10.4324/9781003317333-25

quality: visibility and differentiated costs. As such, people trust what they can see and what they can understand. Naively or not, folks believe that firms won't spend huge amounts of money on environmental R&D if they are not serious about it. In the end, people tend to trust firms which do something that is costly and both highly and easily visible.

In this light, firms have a battery of endeavours to choose from to woo their stakeholders and the biggies, which include environmental patents, board committees dedicated to environmental issues, environmental pay policies, voluntary environmental government schemes, and environmental trademarks. These vary in their visibility and implementation costs and therefore in their potential efficiency for signalling quality.

Strategies under the lens

If we return to the formula that best-practice legit is a combination of highly visible plus differentiated costs, then a perfect example is that of environmental patents. They require firms to invest significant time, effort, and money to conduct research and make them happen and they are granted only after careful examination to ensure the innovation value of the patented product or process. Patent information is also publicly available. Together, these factors make the characteristics of a strong signal: accordingly, people trust them more as they are based upon real effort.

Another example of a strong signal is the existence of environmental committees. These are created within firms specifically for the development and implementation of environmental policies which in turn are subsequently included in a company's annual reports. These are also costly for companies, requiring the creation of new roles, responsibilities, control systems, and sometimes even hiring new board members. A similar story goes for environmental pay policies: their development and implementation require substantial resources while the information about such pay policies is usually included in annual reports. All in all, these three actions constitute powerful ways to create that much sought-after environmental legitimacy – after all, the public wouldn't expect an irresponsible company to make long-term environmental commitments.

On the contrary, actions that do not require substantial investment and that remain in the shadows obviously fail to be effective in building a strong corporate reputation. One such example is that of participating in government-sponsored schemes, very often without any obligation to achieve tangible objectives and results. In the case of the WasteWise programme in the US, for example, no penalties were applied to participants who failed to reach the objective of reducing waste. However, participants were able to publicise their membership of the scheme, regardless of their environmental record – and this allowed the participants' firms to blow green smoke.

Surprisingly, the same can be said of environmental trademarks. No ground-breaking innovation has to be declared and they cost the same for any firm, irrespective of their real environmental performance. Lo and behold, though – almost every producer remembers to stick the magic words 'eco', 'bio', and 'no GMO' on the label. Does this create trust? Maybe not.

Perks and pitfalls

Recent research has focused on these weak and strong signals through the study of 325 large firms operating in the 20 most polluting industrial sectors over a five-year period. Results were gleaned comparing the firms' environmental actions and the following change in their level of legitimacy, measured through responses, external evaluations, certifications, and media accounts.

The study indeed endorses the argument that initiatives involving greater commitment – read visibility and costs – are an effective way to improve corporate reputation. Environmental patents turn out to be the strongest signal. However, other environmental actions increase legitimacy only when the company has strong existing credibility, but they might harm it in other circumstances. This means that firms would be wise not to offer empty promises. Setting up environmental board committees and policies, for example, which later does not lead to real action, weakens trust and might even lead to a downturn in the firm's performance and value if stakeholders and shareholders lose faith. In this light, such attempts at greenwashing can break bonds between firms and their stakeholders – maybe for years, maybe forever.

Enter the NGO

Greenwashing may also backfire from the presence and action of environmental NGOs. These organisations promote environmental values, tending to focus on the shadier side of a firm's footprint than the lighter. More often than not, if a company's environmental performance improves, it stays off the NGO's radar. Give them a scandal or a dose of environmental pollution and NGOs go straight for the throat. As such, greenwashing is a red flag for environmental NGOs, always on their guard – and rightly so – to signal the inconsistency between a firm's claims and real results.

Down the road

Increasing numbers of companies are jumping on the green management bandwagon. In fact, it's difficult nowadays to spot one that isn't. Some use environmental actions and policies to save face and gain approval from their stakeholders and despite their environmental performance being poor. However, a substantial, positive environmental performance is difficult to fake, particularly when the firm operates in an environmentally sensitive sector. And it is here that greenwashing has a good chance of backfiring. The public – the audience of consumers – is very receptive to strong signals and less receptive to weak signals, with one possible exception being green trademarks. What's more, an increasing number of environmental NGOs are tracking any environmental issue or inconsistency with a firm's declared policies. As such, if firms are searching for easy ways to impress stakeholders, it may still be safer for them to do nothing rather than pretend to be green.

Street cred'

Research has focused almost exclusively on large, publicly traded firms, obviously more exposed to public scrutiny. Can smaller companies and private firms get away with environmental actions that fail to match their claims, even in the presence of NGOs? As every year passes, it seems to be less and less likely as environmental concerns have reached their zenith in recent years with information coverage being large and loud. Another important factor is that environmental NGOs are doing a good job in reducing incentives for greenwashing. In the near future, they can potentially further increase their role and impact by also offering greater incentives to achieve better ESG performance. It seems that cosmetic environmental actions and empty promises no longer pay off – and that is a good thing. Being sustainable is now a strategic choice for leaders who want their companies to succeed.

Key takeaways

- Environmental legitimacy is one of the key competitive factors in business. In order to earn stakeholder trust, companies seek to comply with their expectations in the field of environmental responsibility.
- A wide range of environmental actions and policies can be used to build a solid corporate reputation, but not all of them are equally efficient. Two key features of environmental actions that send strong signals of environmental quality are visibility and differentiated costs.
- Actions such as environmental patents, pay policies, and environmental committees have strong signalling power. They require substantial investment in R&D and other costs, which look trustworthy to the public eye.

- On the contrary, green trademarks and participation in government-sponsored environmental schemes with no clear obligations to achieve tangible objectives are weak signals. It is easier to manipulate such signals in order to create a better image.
- Actions that require greater costs and visibility are more likely to be considered authentic by the wider public. Environmental patents constitute the strongest signal as they help firms gain legitimacy, regardless of their credibility. Other environmental actions increase legitimacy only when a company has strong existing credibility, otherwise, false promises can be detrimental to corporate performance and value.
- Greenwashing today is becoming a risky matter. In the presence of environmental NGOs, environmental efforts are difficult to fake as NGOs amplify the inconsistency between corporate claims and their real results.
- Only genuinely green companies can be sure that their environmental signals will build them legitimacy among stakeholders.

Food for thought

- Take a look at the foodstuffs, health and sanitary products, or white and brown goods in your home. Which ones openly claim to be 'good for the planet'?
- To what extent did you consciously buy these products with the planet and the environment in mind?
- Which brands in your country have a strong reputation for being environmentally friendly or responsible? What makes them so? And to what extent do consumers trust them and remain repeat customers?

Related research: *Does Greenwashing Pay Off? Understanding the Relationship Between Environmental Actions and Environmental Legitimacy, August 2017, Journal of Business Ethics 144(2), DOI: 10.1007/ s10551-015-2816-9*

Micro case study 4: Accounting

SuperSuper, part 4

Penelope Super is a young engineer who has worked for a while in a Design Thinking consulting firm in California. Back home, she is the new Director for Innovation. She is now talking with her aunt Pamela, the CFO.

Pamela: We have every reason to be proud of our sustainability reporting. Not only we are constantly appreciated by the press, we are now part of a sustainability index!

Penelope: All that's very nice. But we won't go far with that.

Pamela: What do you mean? Grandpa would've been so proud!

Penelope: Yes, I'm not saying it's bad. Don't get me wrong. It's a good sustainability report, with lots of information. It's reliable – we have it audited by a top firm.

Pamela: So?

Penelope: All that information help us to improve our operations, and be better than our competitors. That's great. But it's not enough. At the end of the day, all those improvements, welcome as they are, are incremental.

Pamela: Can you explain that? Isn't it good to improve?

Penelope: Of course, improving is great. Let's say that we reduce packaging, recycle here and there, and put a few solar panels and the like. Our sustainability will improve, of course. Hats off! But we're keeping the same way of doing things. Who knows, maybe a smarter competitor will disrupt us with a greener, more profitable business model. You know the stories of Motorola, Kodak, and Blockbuster.

Pamela: Come on, you've read too much Clayton Christensen! Supermarkets have existed for ages. This business will never change. And we're part of the sustainability index – this means that we're much better than our competitors.

What do you think? Which advice would you give to Penelope and Pamela? Should the company explore new business models?

You, this book, and your knowledge
A self-assessment tool

1. How much did you know about responsible finance and accounting before reading this book?

   ❑ Very little ❑ Some notions ❑ Knowledgeable and eager to learn more ❑ I practise it

2. After reading this book, what three things will you most likely take away from it? . . . .
. . . .
. . . .
. . . .
. . . .
. . . .
. . . .
. . . .
. . . .
. . . .

3. Which insights in each chapter struck you most? Which were most useful? What knowledge will you most likely remember and take away with you for future use? . . . .
. . . .
. . . .
. . . .
. . . .
. . . .
. . . .
. . . .
. . . .

4. How much would you say about responsible finance and accounting now?

❑ Still very little and I am still not convinced that finance and accounting can be 'responsible' in nature and beneficial to business, people, and planet.

❑ I've learnt quite a bit and want to go deeper into the subject.

❑ I've learnt a lot and I am convinced that this will shape both the sectors covered and my career/career choice.

How can you put this knowledge into action?

❑ In one of my essay assignments.

❑ As part of a student project I have been set.

❑ As the subject of an article I will write for a blog or magazine.

❑ In my internship, apprenticeship, or job.

❑ I will show the book to my fellow students/work colleagues.

❑ I intend to follow a career in green finance or responsible accounting.

Index

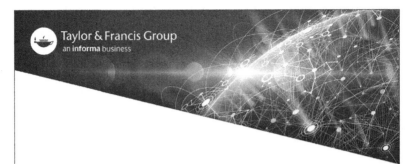

Printed in the United States
by Baker & Taylor Publisher Services